BEYOND THE SILVER RIVER

BEYOND THE SILVER
— RIVER —

South American Encounters

JIMMY BURNS

BLOOMSBURY

First published 1989
Copyright © 1989 by Jimmy Burns

Bloomsbury Publishing Ltd, 2 Soho Square, London W I V 5 D E

British Library Cataloguing in Publication Data
Burns, Jimmy, *1953–*
Beyond the Silver River: South American
Encounters.
1. South America. Description & travel
– Personal observations
I. Title
918'.0438

I S B N 0-7475-0269-2

Photoset by Rowland Phototypesetting Ltd
Bury St Edmunds, Suffolk
Printed and bound in Great Britain by
Butler & Tanner Ltd, Frome and London

During the five years Jimmy Burns was based in Buenos Aires, which resulted in his award-winning study of the Falklands War and its aftermath, *The Land That Lost Its Heroes*, he also embarked on further-flung journeys in Argentina, in Brazil, Peru, Ecuador, Bolivia and Chile. 'Each South American country is idiosyncratic – it brings out our individual fantasies and forces us to interpret anew,' writes Burns. Certainly to travel with him is to trace the footprints of history – conquest and subjugation, defiance and hope – yet to encounter at each turn a fresh observation, the unexpected.

He conducts us by steam train up the Andes and down to the treacherous depths of a Bolivian tin mine. We find a hotbed of Argentine loyalties in Tierra del Fuego, beaches of bodies beautiful in Brazil and Peruvian streets where fanatical Sendero Luminoso guerrillas wage a permanent power struggle with the military. Burns introduces us to Sixto Vázquez, Indian intellectual with an unshakeable faith in legend and animism; to Tina, White Russian Duchess of Platinov, who now presides over an eerie domain of enormous moths in the Ecuadorian rain forest; to Father Renato Hevía, the editor of a Jesuit magazine in Chile who is harassed and detained if he fails to mention Pinochet in even one edition.

'South America remains the least discovered continent,' states Burns. 'Travellers' tales have not tamed it, and therein lies its continuing fascination for those of us who seek a greater understanding.' To this journey of discovery Jimmy Burns brings all the clarity of vision and eloquence of expression for which he was honoured with the 1988 Somerset Maugham Award for Non-fiction.

**TO JULIA AND MIRIAM,
OUR DAUGHTERS BORN IN SOUTH AMERICA**

'. . . he felt an urgent need to escape somewhere from the skyscrapers, the traffic blocks, the sirens of police cars and ambulances, the heroic statues of liberators on horseback . . .'

Graham Greene, *The Honorary Consul*

'Mientras escribo estoy ausente
y cuando vuelvo ya he partido:
voy a ver si a las otras gentes
les pasa lo que a mí me pasa,
si son tantas como soy yo
si se parecen a sí mismos
y cuando lo haya averiguado
voy a aprender tan bien las cosas
que para explicar mis problemas
le hablaré de geografía.'

Pablo Neruda

('While I write I am absent and when I return I have already left; I am going to find out if other people experience the same thing as I do, if they are as many as I am, if they look like each other, and when I have found all this out, I'm going to learn things so well that in order to explain my problems, I'll talk of geography.')

CONTENTS

ILLUSTRATIONS

VENEZUELA

COLOMBIA

GUYANA

SURINAM

FRENCH GUIANA

Esmeraldas
Atacamas
Santo Domingo
Guayaquil

Otavalo
Quito
ECUADOR

Iquitos

PERU

BRAZIL

Lima
Machu Picchu
Cuzco
La Paz
BOLIVIA
Santa Cruz
Sucre
Potosí

Salvador
(Bahia)

La Quiaca
Tilcara
Jujuy
Salta
PARAGUAY
Buzios
Parati
Rio de Janeiro

Tucumán

Pacific
Ocean

Atlantic
Ocean

C

Mendoza
Santiago
H

ARGENTINA

URUGUAY
Buenos Aires

I

Temuco
Valdivia
Puerto Montt
Chiloé

L

Neuquén
San Martín
Bariloche

0   500   1000 km

E

Comodoro Rivadavia

m

Lago Argentino
Rio Gallegos

Ushuaia

PREFACE

My link with South America began more than four hundred years before I was born. An ancestor on my Spanish mother's side, called Marañón, was a member of that army of criminals, romantics and adventurers known as the *conquistadores* who were responsible for the conquest of the Indian populated lands of the New World. He left Spain in 1572 and, lost finally in the impenetrable maze of the Amazon, gave his name to one of the river's two major tributaries. The Rio Marañón flows between the jungle and the Andes across what is today part of northern Peru.

Gregorio Marañón, my maternal grandfather, was a traveller too. In his flat in Madrid, where I was born, there was a library filled with travel books written over the centuries by Spaniards, Englishmen, Italians, Germans and Frenchmen who had made their way across the Atlantic in the footsteps of Don Pedro. 'To understand what travel means', my grandfather used to say, 'you have to follow Don Quixote down into the Cave of Montesinos and fall asleep. Then, when you wake, you will never be quite sure what is real or imagined. But it will be an undeniable experience all the same.'

It was a philosophy my father, Tom, subscribed to from an early age. He was born in Chile, the son of a Scotsman and an Anglo-Chilean. In 1906, when he was only six months old, the roof of his home in a seaside town on the Pacific coast collapsed on top of him during the biggest earthquake Chile had ever had. He was saved from certain death by the timely intervention of his wet nurse – a large woman who managed to spread herself across him before taking the full weight of the falling masonry on her broad back. Miraculously, they both survived.

My parents sent me for my formal education to Stonyhurst in the north of England. This was no ordinary English public school. Gerard Manley Hopkins wrote some of his poetry there and Arthur Conan Doyle, the creator of Sherlock Holmes, was expelled by the Jesuits who ran it. Stonyhurst was therefore a place where anything could happen. Even ghosts. We were told that many ghosts lurked in the college's treasured Arundel library. The Jesuits saw the warning as a way of ensuring that this particular area of the building remained strictly out of bounds to all but the most rebellious. One night, when I was thirteen, I crept down the library's sombre corridors and caught a glimpse of an arrogant figure, holding an alligator under his arm. It was a painting of Charles Waterton, one of the English writers in my grandfather's library – an old Stonyhurst boy who had left for South America in 1812, on the first of several journeys. Waterton's ghost evaded me that night but, in the chill of the library with its priceless treasures and stuffed South American birds, my imagination was further stirred.

Waterton was the first of a line of British explorers who in the last century and the early part of this one travelled to South America. The majority of them, men like W. H. Hudson and Robert Cunningham Graham, did most of their travelling in Argentina, creating a considerable proportion of that country's early literature. Their writings contain a wealth of detail and insight into a little-known territory of the world, and much of it is tinged with the freshness and excitement which comes with exploration.

South America remains the world's least discovered continent. Travellers' tales have not tamed it, and therein lies its continuing fascination. Those of us who have had the fortune to live and work there may touch on some of the same places, encounter similar landscapes, but our reactions will rarely be the same. Each South American country is idiosyncratic – it brings out our individual fantasies and forces us to interpret anew. This book is drawn from the diaries I kept during the five years my wife, Kidge, and I lived in South America. During this period I was working as a journalist in Buenos Aires, although we travelled extensively throughout the continent. Our journeys were usually taken towards the end of the year because this is the summer period in the southern hemisphere, when the days are longest and when Kidge was given time off by her school.

Our visits to Uruguay and Paraguay were always brief, and we returned to London before ever getting to know Venezuela and Colombia. So I have drawn on our experience in six countries – Argentina, Brazil, Peru, Ecuador, Bolivia and Chile, which between them claim to capture the spirit of a continent.

The identities of several characters have been disguised so as not to put them at any kind of risk. My encounters with them were more often than not on the grounds that I was a traveller rather than a journalist and our conversations were those simply between the curious and the enlightened, and not for the record. I have tried wherever possible to stick to a chronology, but the book incorporates thoughts I wrote down in no particular order while living in Buenos Aires, and compresses into the main journey some minor travels that took place at different stages between 1982 and 1985. Though she might seem to have been a silent witness on many of our journeys, I wish to note a special debt to Kidge, a source of constant companionship and inspiration throughout our travels, and to my parents, Tom and Mabel, whose union of cultures made this book possible.

JB

— 1 —

ESCAPE FROM BUENOS AIRES

'Whatever you do,' Jacobo Timerman had told me, just before Kidge and I left London for South America, 'don't start writing about Florida Street. All foreigners begin that way. But that's not Buenos Aires, let alone South America.'

Timerman had only recently been released from an Argentine prison where he had been tortured and told he was a 'Jewish pig'. We had met for lunch in Covent Garden, across the road from the offices of Amnesty International.

'So where do I start?' I asked him.

'In Pompeya,' Timerman said.

And so we started in Pompeya. It was a poor suburb of Buenos Aires, in drab concrete and fading pink, which had nevertheless managed to preserve within its boundaries an image of what the city had once been. The bustle of the old port, from where Argentina had once fed half the world with its grain and beef, had moved to the Mercado del Pájaro, Pompeya's bird market, where men in white overalls haggled over prices and feathers danced and dived amidst the crowds like the remnants of a gigantic pillow fight. More than a century ago, the English naturalist W. H. Hudson, recalling his first visit to Buenos Aires, had marvelled at the gathering of the *lavanderas*, the washerwomen. The ceaseless gabble, mingled with the yells and shrieks of laughter of the black women, had reminded him of the sound made by a 'great concourse of gulls, ibises, godwits, geese, and other noisy water-fowl on some marshy lake' of the *pampa*, the great prairie that spans much of Argentina. The blacks had long since disappeared, exterminated by plagues and wars. But the birds and their vendors in the market in Pompeya seemed to resurrect their spirit.

I returned to Florida Street. There were no birds there, only boutiques and travel agencies, and a large, leatherbound tea-room called the Richmond, where Eduardo Plarr, the doctor in Graham Greene's *The Honorary Consul*, had sat sipping tea with his mother.

It was a street made for pedestrians to look at each other, a permanent fashion show of knowing stares and attitudes.

I never returned to Pompeya. But I did walk down Florida Street many times. It was the short cut from the station to my office in Avenida Córdoba; it was also the centrepiece of the fifteen square blocks around which the capital's political and financial life revolved. Thus I was drawn to the area not so much out of any sense of curiosity or fantasy, but by convenience and professional need. It was not long before Florida Street had worn me down with its pretensions. I came to despise the way it merely aped Europe without ever quite managing to better it, laid claim to represent Argentina only because it took the political and financial decisions, and seemed to turn its back on the rest of Latin American culture. This was the Argentina that European and American businessmen came to and admired before returning home and reporting on what a civilised part of South America they had just been to.

But Florida Street did not really exist. It was an imitation of something else, and even now I cannot recall its smells or colour or sounds. I believe it never had any. When the Galtieri junta carried out the invasion of the Falklands in April 1982, Florida Street was swamped in blue and white flags – the national colours – and martial music and jingles and slogans proclaiming the justice of nationhood and Latin American solidarity. But it all seemed as fraudulent as the fashion show.

The American writer, Paul Theroux, setting off on his travels around Great Britain, remarked from London at the time, 'The longer I lived in London, the more I came to realise how much of Englishness was bluff.' In Buenos Aires, as the Falklands War developed, my feelings about the city I had chosen to live in, mirrored this exactly. The longer I lived in Buenos Aires, the more I came to realise how much of 'Argentinismo' was bluff. The *porteños*, as the inhabitants of Florida Street are called, loudly proclaimed their opinions about Las Malvinas, and yet they seemed to fail so miserably as patriots.

One day in May, at the height of the war, I went to the headquarters of the Argentine navy and said, 'I want to see the Argentina that is not Buenos Aires, where can I go?'

'You cannot go west, you cannot go south, and you cannot go east. You can go north, but only if you're careful and stay away from the Chilean frontier. The Chileans are helping the English,' the navy's press officer said.

So it was not to be a journey without maps. And yet the officer's warning contained a necessary note of realism. I was conscious that in setting out from Buenos Aires in search of the wider continent, Kidge and I were following in the footsteps not of *porteños* but of hardier and more curious English travellers. Long before the Falklands War, they had discovered that South America was not just an exotic land but a place where grim death could also occur.

I remember the muddy River Plate, which divides Argentina from Uruguay, was looking unusually beautiful one dawn in May – an autumn month in the southern hemisphere. Its waters were streaked with silver by the crisp light, and a soothing purity hung over the city, as if this was the first day of its existence. But at the airport we were arrested, initially on grounds of 'insufficient documentation'. The officer who interrogated us wove an intricate conspiracy theory and accused us of being spies. It took about twelve hours of questioning by more senior and experienced officers, an intervention on our behalf by friends in the Foreign Ministry, and the support of Hugh O'Shaughnessy of the *Observer*, acting both as colleague and unofficial lawyer, to have the charges dismissed. Our arrest passed into history as simply one more in a number of similar incidents that occurred throughout the war. But the experience stuck with us. It deepened the paranoia that had stimulated the urge for travel in the first place. Kidge, along with the other English teachers at her school, a few days later caught a boat across the River Plate to temporary exile in Uruguay. I was left thinking more and more of the 'madness, melancholia, and panic fear' which Graham Greene has noted as inherent to the human condition and for which travel, as much as the act of writing, provides a form of therapy. I vowed that once Galtieri had been defeated and I had been reunited with Kidge, we would begin where we had left off, in search of South America, beyond the silver river.

— 2 —

BETWEEN THE MOUNTAINS
AND THE DESERT

The province of Salta stretches from the Andes mountains in the west of Argentina to the flat salt-lands in the east. In between is a rolling countryside of hills and fertile valleys. Salta is believed to have taken its name from a fusion of Indian words, *Sallata*, *sagta*, *sayta* and *sata* meaning a 'beautiful region of hills in whose fertile valley one can find peace'. Looking at the map, it seemed as good a place as any from which to begin our journey.

On the 1,600 kilometres plane-ride north from Buenos Aires, we flew for the first half-hour over the prairie – part of the Argentine *pampa* – which had turned golden beneath the early morning sun. Then the land turned darker, rose and bifurcated, became jagged and sweeping at the same time like waves in a cruel sea. Kidge and I sat on opposite sides of the gangway exchanging vistas. We marvelled at the contrast with the concrete oppressiveness of Buenos Aires and its surrounding flatness. On the right, the hills rose towards snow-capped peaks, barely distinguishable from the cloud formations. On the left they fell and melted into desert. Then the plane dipped and descended over a civilised land of vineyards and orchards in a valley once populated by some of South America's most ancient Indian tribes. The Spanish *conquistadores* had fought and defeated the Indians as they pushed south from Peru and north from Buenos Aires in an effort to unite an Empire. And it was here that Don Hernando de Lerma, Viceroy of Peru, had in 1582 founded the imperial town of Salta.

The Salta we encountered had lost none of its colonial charm. A clear mountain air, touched with the smell of orange groves and peaches, filtered through the luminous streets of whitewashed buildings. In this town of 600,000 people, no one seemed to be in a hurry and at three o'clock in the afternoon *siesta* time was adhered to religiously. Evidence of an ancient imperial splendour lay distributed around its plazas and within its palm-lined gardens. With their sloping tiles, grilled black windows, and sturdy Mozarabic arches, the churches and government offices reminded us of Andalucía.

We lingered in the cathedral, with its huge, late baroque altar defiantly resisting the advent of more humble times, and contemplated the sacred images of Christ and the Virgin which, so legend has it, had saved Salta from being destroyed in an earthquake in the seventeenth century. We stopped by the eighteenth-century convent of San Bernardo with its elaborate and massive wooden portal, and gazed up at the tower of San Francisco, believed to be the tallest in South America. White doves swooped in and out past its bells. Beyond its churches, Salta was filled with statues and monuments of past military heroes and men of learning, but none struck me as much as that of Don Hernando de Lerma. A stocky man with a wispy beard, this nobleman from Seville clutched his cloak and armour and, head raised, surveyed the city with an attitude of supreme arrogance. The statue was not just a reminder of a more glorious past, it was also an image of social distinction. In Salta to be of Spanish stock was to be a class above all others.

Pedro, the taxi-driver who had picked us up at the airport, belonged to the opposite end of the social scale. With his dark olive skin, high cheekbones, and jet-black hair, he was a half-caste, a diluted descendant of the Diaguitas. This tribe had lived in the Calchaquí valley around Salta centuries before the first Spaniard set foot in Argentina, but had long since been subjugated. Next to Pedro, in the front seat of his 1950s Peugeot, crouched Mercedes, his three-year-old daughter. Physically, she had inherited his features, but whereas Pedro was sullen, Mercedes was effervescent. From the moment he had heard my Castilian accent, he had assumed an air of servility which no amount of effort on my part could dispel. He avoided my eyes in conversation and bowed his head with every phrase he uttered. Mercedes, on the other hand, seemed refreshingly indifferent to my status. She was holding a piece of chocolate which now and then she would lick like a puppy. For most of the time she fiddled with a rosary and a chain of Saint Christopher, the patron saint of travellers, which dangled from the ignition keys, and giggled outrageously at the passing statues. 'Salta was one of the first cities to be founded by imperial Spain,' Pedro started monotonously when I asked him what it was like to live there. He then talked quickly, covering a people's entire history in less than a minute.

'Following the seventeenth and eighteenth centuries, it became a very important staging post for the imperial commerce that went all the way from the Atlantic Ocean across the Andes to the Pacific. The grandsons and great-grandsons of those first Spaniards were good warriors and became the heroes of our independence from Spain in the nineteenth century. You have heard of General Güemes, I trust. But Buenos Aires became the capital, and much power and money left Salta for the south after the collapse of the old Empire. Today, as you can see, some of us are poor, but the old great Spanish families of Salta – they are in charge of much of our industry and agriculture. They live in big estates, out of town, and have good horses . . . '

'Can you take me to a phone?' I interrupted. I had been given the name of one of these families before setting out from Buenos Aires. The family owned a sugar refinery, orchards and several herds of cattle. They were among the richest in Argentina. But when I rang, a servant told me that his masters were in Europe, on holiday. The card warning of our arrival had either been misplaced or simply ignored.

'Is there much absenteeism here?' I asked Pedro, while Mercedes smudged her chocolate on the car window. '*Bueno*,' Pedro said. (*Bueno* does not mean good in this part of the world. It is not really a word. It is a punctuation, a playing for time, like the English 'errrr'.)

'*Bueno, Señor*,' Pedro said again, turning his eyes away from the mirror so as to avoid my eyes, 'I am not really the right person to ask about these things. I am simply a taxi-man, a working man.'

Pedro, Mercedes, Kidge and I spent the rest of the afternoon together, driving round Salta at *siesta* time. Several shops we passed had huge posters on their windows: 'LAS MALVINAS SON ARGEN-TINAS,' they proclaimed against the background of a giant-sized soldier placing the national flag on top of a mountain. The radio station which Pedro had tuned into was regularly interrupted with excerpts of the military anthem that had accompanied Argentine troops throughout their occupation of the islands. The military junta was still insisting that only a battle had been lost, not a war. But the war was over here in Salta, it really was. Pedro knew it and I knew it, but the two of us had said all we had to say. Mercedes was now sleeping curled up against her father's right-hand pocket, chocolate and a mop of long black hair criss-crossing her face like war paint. Awake, weathered features and self-assurance had given Mercedes the appearance of a spent woman. In sleep she had regained the innocence of an angel. It was July, a winter month, but the air was dry and hotter than it had been in Buenos Aires. In England, the weather was a topic of idle conversation. Here it made me think of the young

Salteños, younger than myself, who had been sent to Las Malvinas only to freeze to death.

My other contact in Salta was Spain's honorary Consul. The Spanish Consulate was perched on a hill, along an avenue lined with ceibo trees. Near it stood a statue of Christopher Columbus, somewhat out of place in a suburb of custom-built houses, made for the town's nascent bourgeoisie. It was five o'clock when we arrived at the Consulate. Here, as in the centre, Salta was somnolent. There was a large grey cat sleeping in the sun but otherwise no sign of life. The Consulate door had a 'Closed for Business' sign. I pressed the bell. The cat stirred as Kidge fondled it, arched its back, and then paced in slow motion to another place in the sun before collapsing again. From inside the building a hoarse male voice issued a curse. Then there were the sounds of a cupboard opening and shutting, a rattling of plates and two feet dragging towards us across a carpetless floor.

'What the devil is going on? The Consulate is closed, can't you read the sign?' the voice said from the other side. Then the door opened, revealing a short, barrel-shaped figure of a man. He stood bleary-eyed and somewhat puffy in his shorts after what I took to have been an interrupted siesta. I gave him my visiting card and introduced myself as the nephew of Gregorio Marañón, Franco's last Ambassador to Buenos Aires.

'I am the Consul, but for the love of God don't call me Honorary Consul or Eminence or Don anything, no one who is in the least friendly in this country calls me that. Call me plain Pepe. I'm Pepe and nothing more,' he said.

Inside the Consulate, there appeared to be only one room that was remotely functional. It had a desk, a typewriter, a telephone and a portrait of King Juan Carlos. Pepe ushered us quickly through it as if it contained something disagreeable and didn't stop until we had entered his living quarters. Then a huge smile came over his face. 'This is where I can relax,' he said.

The room smelt faintly of wine and olive oil, although the only trace of food or drink was a half-empty glass of water and a piece of ham. The remains of Pepe's lunch were on a small coffee table beneath a portrait of Franco. The old dictator's humourless expression was flanked on one side by an engraving of Isabel la Católica, the fifteenth-century monarch who had expelled the Moors from Spain, and on the other by the stuffed head of a bull. 'I call them the three grandees of Spain,' Pepe said.

I asked him about the photograph of a young football player that was on a desk surrounded by flowers. 'That's me in my youth. I used to play for Sevilla football club.'

We followed Pepe into a third room where the smell of wine and olive oil was more intense. Again, there was little in it, except for a large cupboard. 'Here, let me show you my recipe for dealing with inflation,' said Pepe.

The cupboard was filled with boxes of Scotch whisky, racks of wine bottles, and long curved hooks from which hung an assortment of hams, *chorizos* and cheeses. He opened a bottle of wine. 'It's a Rioja, the real stuff, bottled in Spain like what you get in Europe.' Pepe's eyes had lost their bleariness and were now glowing.

As we ate and drank, Pepe told me a Spaniard's story. He had been sent as a young man to Argentina by his family. An uncle, who had emigrated many years before, had written to his parents telling them that on the plains of Argentina, the *pampa*, you could grow what you liked and there was enough land for everyone. It was the land of opportunity, a deliverance from the Spain of the 1930s which was so stark and troubled and hopeless. 'Back in my *pueblo*,' said Pepe, 'I used to watch my folks bent double year in year out just to make one vegetable grow. But on the *pampa* you sat back and watched the seasons come and go, making everything fruitful,' Pepe said.

He did not spend much time on the *pampa*, though. There were not so many jobs and the land belonged to others, so he took a train to Salta where some of his relatives lived. 'I then did what other Spaniards do in Salta. I enjoyed myself while working hard at every-thing I could lay my hands on until I was rewarded as honorary Consul,' he concluded, pouring out some more wine, and passing us some *tapas*. Pepe's real history was probably more complex than this. The portrait of Franco smacked of militarist sympathies, and it was hard to imagine, looking at him now, that this Pepe was the same Pepe that had once been a football star.

William Hudson had this to say about the first Spaniards who had made their homes in this country:

They came from a land where the people are accustomed to sit in the shade of trees, where corn and wine and oil are supposed to be necessaries and where there is salad in the garden. Naturally they made their gardens and planted trees, both for shade and fruit, wherever they built themselves a house ... and no doubt for two or three generations they tried to live as if in Spain in the rural districts. But now the main business of their lives was cattle raising ... and as the cattle roamed at will over the vast plains and were more like wild than domestic animals, it was a life on horseback. They could no longer dig or plough the earth and protect their crops from insects and birds and their own animals. They gave up their oil and wine and bread and lived on flesh alone. They sat in the shade and ate the fruit of trees planted by their fathers or their great-grandfathers until the trees died of old age, or were blown down or killed by the cattle, and there was no more shade and fruit.

Had Hudson been alive to join us on that hot afternoon in Salta, he would have perhaps considered Pepe a survivor, the quintessential inhabitant of the new Argentina.

When, as we left, I asked Pepe if there was much absenteeism, he looked at me with a glint in his bulldog eyes. 'You're a Spaniard, you should know, we're all hard working but we also enjoy life.'

We drove back down to the town, satiated on Pepe's Rioja and his *chorizos*. Salta had woken from its afternoon slumbers and settled into a communal bustle in its plazas and gardens. I thought of England. Here there were no grannies locked away in old people's homes or children sent to bed early. The crowded cafés involved old and young alike in a seemingly timeless festivity. That night we were lulled to sleep in a small back-street *pension* by the distant sound of music and laughter and the scent of eucalyptus creeping through our grilled window.

The next day, we caught an old steam train called *El Tren de las Nubes* – the Train of the Clouds. The round trip took eight hours to cover just over 200 kilometres up into the mountains and back to Salta, and all the way the engine huffed and puffed like an ancient ox. We found our reserved seats at dawn in a wooden carriage that smelt of fruit and tobacco. Opposite me sat two middle-aged spinsters from Buenos Aires. María Ángeles, the fatter of the two, had a pince-nez that hung loosely round the tip of a long nose. She was using it to read a breviary. The other, María Dolores, had a small face that peered mouselike from beneath a soufflé of bleached blonde hair. She was gazing vacantly out of the window while sharing a box of chocolates with her friend. Across the passageway sat a child with his parents, and, opposite them, a young couple, hands clasped, legs entwined, cheek to cheek in an attitude of spent passion.

On the outskirts of Salta, a group of labourers in pale shirts stood motionless by the railway track. We passed the overgrown ruins of a cement factory where a dog was eating the remains of a chicken. On a wall someone had written: 'DIOS ES LA ÚNICA ESPERANZA' ('God is our one hope'). Then the train was making its way across stark hills, littered with the phallic shapes of giant cacti. At times the plants that rose from the brow of a hill were metamorphosed in the early light and became Indian spirits waiting to ambush us. The sky was turquoise, and the horizon, with the jagged outlines of the Andes beyond, seemed cut with a razor.

The train was being pulled backwards up a steep gradient, through a pocket of low cloud. The noise of the steam engine was muffled. Gelatinous drops of evaporation formed on the windows. When we passed a sign by the track saying 3,500 metres, María Ángeles interrupted her prayers and announced she was going to the lavatory. A few minutes later she returned. She was clutching a handkerchief and looking a yellow shade of green. María Dolores began to dab her forehead with a perfumed sponge. 'The bathroom . . . it's a disgrace,' said María Ángeles. Across the passageway, the parents were sitting quietly surrounded by chocolate wrappers and torn comics. The child was vomiting into his mother's lap. In the corner, the young couple was still sleeping.

Down the train, the conductor – a dwarfish fifty year old with a Zapata moustache – was walking quickly. As he was about to pass the spinsters, María Ángeles leaned over and clutched him with her huge hands. 'Inspector, we have been on this train for the best part of a day and all we have seen are Indians and cacti. You call this the Train of the Heavens, but I'm sure, Jesus will forgive me, hell was never like this,' she boomed.

'It's the Train of the Clouds, *Señora*, not the Train of the Heavens,' said the conductor. He had managed to squirm out of reach of her long arms and was now rearranging the silver buttons on his grey jacket. His eyes were darting from one passenger to the other in a silent plea for help. 'The train is having to go more slowly than usual because we are behind a military convoy. The military take precedence over everything, choose the time of arrival, the speed, the stops . . . '

'*Hijos de puta* are those that govern this country. Screw those fucking shits,' said the boy, after disengaging himself from his girl-friend. She too had woken, and was giggling.

'The military says we have to wait and that is what we are doing, waiting. You understand, don't you?' said the conductor.

'The bathroom, it's a disgrace,' said María Ángeles.

'The bathroom is not my responsibility, *Señora*. It's the men higher up. They have the money but not the will to change things. You understand, don't you?' Without waiting for an answer, the conductor bowed his head and walked away as quickly as he'd come.

During the rest of the journey, the child was sick again, María Ángeles went to the bathroom several more times, the couple went back to sleeping in the corner, and the conductor reappeared only once. Going up, the train went from one steep gradient to another, in a complicated push–pull manoeuvre involving two engines and constant switching of tracks, but the Andes never seemed to get any closer and there was little relief from the barren hills. Once, when we had reached the highest point of the tour, over 4,000 metres up, we were allowed to get off the train. The air was very thin, making us gasp for breath. The ground fell sharply away on both sides towards a canyon of yellowish dust. The clouds had cleared.

As I stood looking at the wasted landscape, an old Indian walked over and said, 'Do you see the canyon down there? It used to have everything . . . silver, gold . . . but now there is nothing left.' Then he stood there, looking at the canyon in silence.

Kidge asked him about the railway and he said it had been designed by *los Ingleses* and built by *los Bolivianos*. She asked him what he thought about the war the English had fought with Argentina over Las Malvinas. 'A war with the English? Las Malvinas, you say? . . . I don't know anything about that although I heard once that something had been going on.' Then the train blew its whistle. Its initial sound was like a clarion call. It frightened the Indian traders that lined the railway track and prompted the tourists into a frenetic scramble towards the carriages. Then the whistle reverberated in diminishing echoes across the hills until, once deep into the canyon, it was finally extinguished. The train started to move slowly, picking up speed down the ancient track back towards Salta, breathing heavily as it went.

The next morning we hired a car and began to drive towards the Bolivian border, which lay some 400 kilometres north of Salta. The road was soon taking us through saline hills rising in a dramatic sweep of coloured stone and dust towards the sharp line of the horizon and a deep blue sky. The colours were the most varied we had ever seen in a single landscape. At the base of the hills, the land was a swirling mass of golden yellow which gradually rose in darkening shades to a border of reddish hue. Then the hills became steeper in crumpled ridges of pale and dark blues, before touching the skyline in a purple haze. Now and then we saw in the distance the remnants of Indian villages, the ruined sandstone huts almost hidden in the complex camouflage and containing few signs of life. In over three hours' driving the only living thing we encountered was a giant eagle gliding down towards the valley, and a pair of white horses pacing the hills as if in slow motion. Further on, the powdery sandstone was covered by fields of coarse grass, and the landscape achieved a uniformity of green on ashen grey. Across the horizon, the tops of cacti plants reappeared, their look of spying Indians now complete.

Our Argentine guidebook recommended that along the way we should make a stopover in Jujuy, another old colonial town, which enjoys its own micro-climate and lies completely surrounded by wooded hills. But we gave up the idea unanimously as soon as we touched its outskirts. This onetime Indian stronghold now had a large regiment of conscript soldiers encamped at its entrance. This was certainly not the first army barracks we had seen in Argentina, one of the most militarised societies in South America, but it was the first since leaving Buenos Aires. We drove on quickly, letting the road take us higher up the backbone of South America.

Tílcara is an Indian town surrounded by strange fables. As we approached it that evening, the sun was dipping behind the hills. For an instant its rays rested on a white horse. We stopped the car and watched the animal, still as a statue, grow luminous in the night. A few hundred yards down the road two women covered in shawls were crouching in a ditch. As I walked towards them, they got up and ran away. In the place where they had been, I found a skull, the hollows of the eyes illuminated by a lighted candle. Near by was a roughly stacked pile of coca leaves. We drove into Tílcara along a muddy track lined with squat stone houses steaming from the heat of the pigs and cows that shared their living quarters with their owners. The streets were bathed in the yellowish light of old lamps. Once an old woman, dressed in what seemed to be a black cape, walked out of a hut, crossed the track, and quickly ran through another doorway.

'She's the Black Widow,' Pereira said. 'No one knows if she really exists. But they say she brings bad luck. She has long fingernails painted with silver.'

Pereira was an old professor of folklore whose name I had been given in Buenos Aires. He had a mane of white hair swept back from his forehead, and a strong, youthful face at odds with the rest of his body. When we first encountered him, he was slouched in a velvet armchair in a small dark library, and he rose with difficulty to greet us. I asked him about the two women by the roadside.

'They were almost certainly *curanderas* checking on a lover's fortunes,' he said, breathing heavily once he had slouched back into his armchair. 'The skulls are put there by those who have been abandoned by their partners. Usually they'll put a pair of gold coins in the hollows and leave them there for a month. If at the end of this period, the partner has not returned, the skull will be turned round facing away from the road, the gold coins will disappear, and the coca leaves will burn. It will be a curse then,' Pereira explained.

'But what if the lover does return?' Kidge asked.

'Oh, then the flowers will grow out of the hollows.'

I asked him about the candles.

'There were no candles but only your refusal to see. The skull had turned away and was burning,' Pereira said.

That night we slept in a converted granary with rooms the size of monastic cells. We got into a bed covered with llama wool, thinking about Tílcara's mysteries, and did not move until the next morning.

Pereira had told us that Tílcara had become a town of children, women and old men. 'The desire of individuals to seek a better life materially clashes with the reality of a world economy that has less to offer,' he said. The young men had gone off to find work in the sugar plantations of Tucumán or in the mines of Bolivia. Others had gone as far as Europe. 'When they get there they realise that things are even worse so they come back, although not to their own town – they're too proud for that.' Pereira believed that health was the only area of activity in which the Old and the New World had managed to achieve a compromise, for in Tílcara the *curandera* often worked side by side with the local doctor. No one wanted to live or die with only one or the other, he said.

In the town square there were neither *curanderas* nor doctors. But there were some open stalls filled with flutes and ponchos and plastic skulls. The 'market' had been set up quickly, in time for the arrival of a busload of tourists from Buenos Aires. The tourists now walked around blowing the flutes, trying on the ponchos, and sticking their fingers through the hollows of the skulls. One of the vendors, an old man with torn trousers and yellow teeth, sat smoking a hand-rolled cigarette and holding a radio. He was tuned into the national pop station. The millionaire pop group Abba were singing about the abundance of money in a rich man's world. From the vendor's look of boredom, I suspected that the irony was lost on him.

Near by, next to a church, a group of Indian children was playing with a football. We stood and watched as one of the tourists, a middle-aged woman wearing huge tinted glasses, went up to them and took a photograph. 'How about a little smile?' she said, and took another photograph. 'Well, I suppose you never smile, *pobrecitos*,' she said. She reached into her tight pants and took out a wad of 1,000 peso notes. Theatrically, she fingered the notes and counted to ten. She then looked at the children and, pointing her finger, counted again. Out of the ten children, she picked on one and gave him all the notes. He was the smallest, probably not more than seven years old. He had a dirty face and black eyes and bony little legs. He had played football better than Maradona. But now he stood before the woman, expressionless and silent. He held out his right hand and took the money and then he stared at the notes without flinching. The woman said, 'But don't you know what that is? That's more than your daddy makes in a year. Come now, come with me to the square, let's see what we can buy you.' And the children followed, leaving us with the emptied frame of a white church at sunset.

In the square that evening, we came across Pereira. He was sitting on a bench, leaning on a walking stick. He looked half asleep. I wanted to tell him about the tourists but he told me, as if mesmerised, about *el duende*. He said, 'Watch out tonight for *el duende*, he's a little dwarf with one hand made of leather and the other made of wool. If you don't like him, you slap and punch the leather. If you take to him, stroke the wool softly and lovingly.'

We were standing by Tílcara's equivalent of a village hall. A wooden platform had been erected and surrounded with sheets and rugs held together with clothes pegs. This was the improvised theatre for Tílcara's Festival of Folklore. Inside, the audience was made up of local people wrapped in blankets and eating crisps. On the stage a man was telling a joke about the different forms of copulation of cows and cats. He was dressed in a long tunic and was being followed around by a woman dressed like a tramp. She was dragging a toy machine-gun along the floor and wearing a helmet covered in bullet holes. At one point, the man came over to the woman and stuck a finger in the helmet. The man groaned, took out the finger, and then began walking around the stage, holding himself. The woman screamed after him, 'I'm sorry I'm so tight, but they shot me in the Malvinas.' The joke was greeted with a few nervous giggles. One or two of the older men walked out. And then Kidge noticed him. The little boy who had taken the money that afternoon was laughing hysterically, and in the semi-light his head seemed to grow almost bigger than his body. We could have looked for his hands to see if he was *el duende*. But instead we too left the tent at the interval, and Tílcara that evening.

We decided to spend the night at Humahuaca, the last village sign-posted on the map before the blank space that separates Argentina from Bolivia. It took less than an hour to get there and it was light for most of the way. We passed an Indian graveyard scattered over the edge of a hill – a mass of crooked crosses and broken stones stretched out over the arid earth like the improvised burials of a battlefield. There was an emptiness about the place; there were no inscriptions and only a few parched flowers had been strewn around the tombstones like an afterthought. I looked around the desolate landscape. The sun was going down over the mountains and there were shadows along the horizon where Indian armies had marched five centuries before. It seemed a world apart from the white man's cemetery. I thought of the marble mausoleums of Buenos Aires with their Latin inscriptions and lush trees and bouquets where even Borges was overawed by 'so many noble certainties of dust', by the sheer presence of ceremony and manners, in death as in life.

On the outskirts of Humahuaca, near the banks of a brown river, we stumbled on an open-air market. 'Vendo estereo,' said a Bolivian in cowboy boots, as he blocked our path with a radio. He told me he had brought it all the way from the United States although he looked as if he might not have travelled much further than the border. Next to him, an old grandmother, with long grey hair tied in a black handkerchief and a pipe in her mouth, sat witchlike behind an open box filled with small bags of herbs. There seemed to be not an affliction in the world that could not be remedied by her little display of magic. There was a herb for inflated bladders, a herb for constipation, a herb for bad liver and kidney stones, a herb for hair loss, a herb for impotence. This one promised dreams, that one simple sleep. On the edge, a small bundle of blue flowers guaranteed eternal love. 'I'd like one of each,' Kidge said. The old woman gave us this and more in a large bag. As we were about to leave with our herb garden, she produced from beneath her billowing skirt, a small bottle containing a greenish substance. 'Take it,' she said with a wicked smile, 'frog's juice will give you new life.' We never got to test any of them out. As we pushed our way through the market, two urchins moving in the opposite direction snatched the bag from Kidge's hands, thinking no doubt that it contained a radio. We tried to follow them but lost them in the crowds. The old woman too had disappeared by the time we got to the place where we had first met her. We walked across the bridge, where the dust turned to cobbled stones. There was a festive air in Humahuaca, not the sad improvisation of Tílcara, but a more traditional festivity of church bells and coloured lights and couples courting in the plaza. The *pensión* we stayed at was built around a courtyard filled with geraniums. The place was touched with their sweet-sharp smell. The landlord was an old Spaniard who offered us a glass of wine when Kidge said Humahuaca reminded her of Toledo.

We walked across the village in search of one Sixto Vázquez. Unlike most of the towns and villages in northern Argentina, Humahuaca had been ignored by Buenos Aires University's Department of Archaeology. Because the military had judged it to be too isolated to be of any interest to the average tourist, the village had been left largely in the care of its local inhabitants. There were no reconstructed Indian sites here, just erudite professors like Sixto Vázquez, who shared the secrets of the place only if he trusted you. Sixto belonged to a rare species in Argentina: the Indian who had managed to overcome racial prejudice and class repression through the power of his own intelligence and ambition. Born in a mud hut, he had taught himself to read and write. As a young man he had written a long article about the Indians of the north and sent it to a contact he had been given in Buenos Aires – the features editor on the mass-circulation paper *Clarín*. At the time, in common with much of the media in Argentina, the newspaper was heavily dependent on the State for advertising and permission to publish. It was a time when the military was preparing itself for one of its periodic tactical withdrawals from power and looking for ways of ingratiating itself with the population. Word went out from the highest quarters that the occasional article with social contact would be seen in a good light. Sixto's article arrived on the editor's desk soon after one of these instructions had been received. It was published immediately, generating in its wake a debate in the letters and opinion columns about the place of the Indian in Argentine society. Sixto was adopted as a visiting Professor of Archaeology – or some such title – by the University of Buenos Aires, before returning to Humahuaca as the village's most honoured son.

In recent years Sixto had started up a museum where, in three rooms, the daily life of the local Indian was re-created for the benefit of the curious traveller. The first room had a wax model of an Indian woman brewing a pot of coca tea; the second contained some wax children playing with stuffed reptiles and an assortment of bows and arrows. The third was filled with vegetables, green bottles and an effigy of the devil. Pasted up on the walls were calendars, charts, pictures of Indians fishing, hunting and cooking, but mostly photo-copies of newspaper articles written by Sixto. Pinned to one of them was a photograph of Sixto dressed in a white pyjama suit (one of the Indian festive suits, he told us later) and standing next to two very American-looking travellers in khaki shorts and fat-soled walking shoes.

That afternoon Sixto drove us in his old Dodge up into the hills. When the three of us were standing on the edge of a ridge looking out over the dry valley and the snowy peaks of the Andes on the horizon, he breathed in long and deep. 'You can't see much but you can imagine, almost feel it. Do you see that track over there? That is what is left of the road used by the Incas, from here to Ecuador, half-way across the continent,' he said.

Down in the valley a solitary figure of a man was bent under the weight of a sack of something which looked like dried grass. He was being led by a donkey. The Andes were as distant and intangible as the planets. Sixto was immaculate in his white pyjama suit. He looked like an extra from a cowboy film. I wanted to ask Sixto what he was imagining, what it was he could almost feel. But I didn't say a word.

'You can imagine what it was like when my people ruled over the valley,' he said. He then scratched the ground with his foot and from the rubble extracted a broken piece of pottery. 'This could be five hundred years old,' he said, holding the jagged clay against the sun like a relic. He explained that we were standing on the site of a *pucará*, a fortress, which had been destroyed in the seventeenth century after a long siege by the Spaniards. The few Indians who had survived had been forced into the valley, where they had built a church and founded a new town on the site of what is today Humahuaca.

'Come to supper,' Sixto had said. So we joined him in a room above the museum. It was filled with Indian rugs and Mexican hats, but its most striking feature was an electric Virgin Mary. It blinked over the fireplace, like a traffic light. Over a supper of beans in hot chilli sauce, served silently by his wife, he argued that the only way an Indian community such as Humahuaca's could survive the onslaught of technology and consumerism was to isolate itself culturally and socially and stick firmly to its traditions. Sixto found that the basic dilemma emerged when it came to writing an indigenous novel or short story. 'And by indigenous I mean not writing about Indians but writing as an Indian about Indians in Spanish, the one language that will ensure the widest readership. It is like an oil painter having to use chalk to convey a quintessential expression. Sometimes the language fails the concept. Take the phrase "to love". In Spanish I would have to use *amar*. But the Indian has at least eight different words to express the word "love" in all its feelings and contexts. So how can one express the thoughts of one with the language of another?'

I suggested his Indians were no longer part of the traditional world but an integral cog in a much wider machine, half-way to being absorbed by the market economy. I also argued that no community could talk simply in terms of surviving culturally if it did not have also an idea of its own political and social organisation. 'A ruined *pucará* and a market place selling flutes and herbal mixtures for inflated livers does not make up a society,' I said.

Sixto frowned, his angular face deep in shadow. 'I am only interested in the meaning of existence, and as far as this is concerned I know Indian values matter more than the white man's, however downtrodden my people may seem,' he said. As an *indigenista*, Sixto believed that the Indians' legends, beliefs and animism were indestructible.

Over coffee I asked him why the Indians in Bolivia had betrayed Che Guevara to the military and sent him to his death. Sixto said, 'Guevara failed in Bolivia because he was a white man. What's worse he was an Argentine white man.'

The next morning we went to Mass in a church built by the Jesuits soon after the destruction of the *pucará*. Its walls were thick and ornamental, panelled in gold-covered wood, with huge paintings of saints and an agonised Christ covered in dark red pigment. The Indians making up the congregation were almost indistinguishable in the half-light, huddled together in an attitude of resignation. They recited prayers monotonously like Muslims. The priest had long hair and a beard and celebrated Mass with his arms held out, as if on a cross. He was one of seventeen priests who had to cover an area the size of England and Wales. Each had to walk for days and nights to reach the isolated mountain villages and mining hamlets.

After Mass, the young priest told me that the two most common illnesses were tuberculosis and syphilis. 'Monsignor María Márquez, our Bishop, has organised a voluntary health scheme to help out those afflicted because Buenos Aires doesn't send enough doctors,' said the priest, whom the villagers called Padre Francisco.

In the days when the Indians lived behind the *pucará*, diseases like tuberculosis and syphilis were unknown. They were brought by the Spaniards and spread through their plunder and rape. Then there were other Padre Franciscos who had blessed the conquest as a Crusade of Christ. And now the mission was having to make amends for the curse it had originally blessed. Padre Francisco was at last struggling on behalf of his people.

We drove on towards Bolivia across a desert. There was nothing there except for mud huts without windows and herds of llamas with mangy coats. As we passed, they turned their noses up and sniffed the air. It was as if Argentina had stopped in Humahuaca. The border town of La Quiaca seemed to have been partly converted into a no man's land. Its wide streets were deserted and most of its buildings were boarded up. Crossing the semi-desert, we had choked on the dust and heat, and then, when the sun went down, it became very cold. We stopped off at a hotel near a frontier post. It was filled with people wasting time. They slouched in deep armchairs watching TV and drinking beer. When I asked for the dining room, the landlord looked at me in amazement. 'You want to eat?' he asked.

We were fed on fried eggs and chips and a large jug of red wine. The landlord stood beside a pillar watching us. He couldn't have been more than forty but his face was dark and pock-marked.

'Is it always as cold as this?' I asked.

'Go to the cinema. There's an acceptable film on tonight and you won't be cold there,' he said.

He used the word acceptable which in Spanish can have a range of meanings, from adequate to suitable.

When we got to the cinema I realised why the streets had been so empty. The place was packed: old men snoring, women wrapped in ponchos, children curled up on the floor. Down the passageways there were rows of butane gas fires which bathed the place in a blue glow and projected demonic shapes on to the walls. It was difficult to follow the film because it was an old print, torn and yellow at the edges, and the sound was out of synch. The evening's entertainment was *The Magnificent Seven*, the classic Western about a group of outlaws who cross the border into Mexico and liberate a local peasant community.

The Mexicans looked very like the majority of the people in the audience, and the landscape everyone rode across was like the semi-desert after Humahuaca. So it didn't much matter that the speech of the Seven's leader, played by Yul Brynner, came thirty seconds after his mouth moved and that he was still talking when his face had disappeared.

The film projector broke down four times, leaving the cinema in temporary darkness. No one protested. Perhaps they were used to it or felt too cold to worry. In the real west, *The Magnificent Seven* had been a box-office hit. But here on the Bolivian border people were too cold to worry either way.

The Bolivian side of the border had a market selling live chickens, sweet potatoes and Japanese stereos. We sat in a café. Its only other occupant was an Indian woman with a broad-brimmed hat and long black pigtails. She was bent double over a bowl of soup, slurping. When she looked up she said, 'Bolivia bad country, go back to Argentina.' Kidge asked her to explain, but she went on drinking her soup before falling asleep on the table. We walked down a street filled with foreign exchange booths where men in tight jeans beckoned, brandishing paper money. Near a newspaper stand, a boy with a scar on his face offered us some cocaine. Further on, a group of men in long capes were watching a cock fight. There was a train leaving for La Paz in about five hours' time. A bus was leaving earlier on the same route, but was already packed with people. The boy who had offered us cocaine asked if we wanted a taxi. We decided we would leave Bolivia for another trip, enter it through another frontier, when we had more time on our hands to try and understand a country that on this occasion at least seemed to conspire against us.

We walked back across the border to Argentina. Over the next week, we made our way back towards Buenos Aires. Beyond the desert, we drove through the sugar plantations of Tucumán and followed the hidden paths that lead to the tropical hills. Across the fields, men stripped to their waists slashed through the sugar cane with glistening *machetes* or sat in carts, dazed and worn. Now and then we passed the metallic structure of a refinery, like an old steamer adrift, billowing black smoke. The low clouds came down over the road, closed in, dulled and diminished the landscape. It was warm and damp and dark and very sinister.

It was here in the 1970s the young middle-class students from Buenos Aires had taken time off from their studies in an attempt to bring the Guevarist theory of revolution to the striking sugar workers. Tucumán was more like Cuba than Bolivia ever was, but the revolution was betrayed all the same. The young *guerrilleros* were captured in droves down in the valley. They were tortured and raped and stuck together with pieces of gelignite before being blown up. Bits of body then fertilised the plantations along with the bird shit. Under the military, Tucumán had earned the dubious distinction of having founded the 'institution' of the secret detention camp to house the first 'disappeared'.

The camp run by the military was called the Little Schoolroom because it was built on the site of a school. The prisoners were brought there in unmarked cars, either in the boot or lying on the floor. A red band was tied round the necks of those sentenced to death. Every night a lorry used to arrive to pick up the condemned and take them to the sugar refinery, which had been temporarily transformed into an extermination camp. The few who escaped retreated up into the hills. They never came down again but were killed off in small groups by machine-gun fire, mortar bombs and napalm. I had been told that in the jungle now lay hundreds of skeletons – yesterday's psychoanalysts and doctors – in death as in life clutching their theories on revolution in the quiet shade of the monkey trees. Had I not been told about the local history, it would have been difficult to imagine that anything out of the ordinary had happened in Tucumán. The refineries were in full commercial production again, and the Little Schoolroom had been bulldozed. Only one or two of the houses that lined the highway suggested that something unusual might have occurred there once upon a time. Their occupants had painted the outside walls in the now fading blue and white colours of the national flag to identify their loyalty to the military. There were no formal monuments to the soldiers, though, and that at least was gratifying. For the spirits lurking in the jungle had gained their own special kind of historical justice: General Mario Benjamín, who had commanded the anti-guerrilla operations in the 1970s, had returned to Argentina in disgrace in 1982 after losing the Falklands War.

All the same, we were anxious to put a huge distance between ourselves and Tucumán. We drove through the mutilated cane fields, and up through hills of creeping undergrowth where the air was humid. Eventually the forest opened on to fields filled with vines, some entwined in trellises, others cropped close to the ground and held in place by wires. We were in the Cuyo region, one of the best wine areas in South America.

We drove on, in the direction of the rocky eastern slopes of the Andes, which now rose on the horizon. As we moved towards them, the mountains multiplied and grew, and we saw that the higher peaks were covered in snow. By early evening we were following the highway through Argentina's skiing resorts. Even at this late hour, the slopes were covered with holiday makers. After the rural primitiveness of the cane fields, we had entered a world of fashion. Briefly we stopped and watched hundreds of Argentines sliding in and out between each other with their mirrored sunglasses, blue anoraks, and bright red slacks. Here and there a woman skier was dressed all in white, or all in yellow, and a male instructor wore a hat with louder stripes than the others. Everywhere children and beginners were clomping across the snow like penguins. As I watched them, I had the impression that no one was skiing with real enjoyment, but because it was expected.

We drove back along the highway and stopped off for the night at the only hotel we could find beyond the immediate confines of the resort. Architecturally it was a graceless place – a mock *château* filled with piped music and plastic furniture. But it offered its clients a spectacular view of the mountains. We watched the evening sun set behind the snow peaks, then the snow turning cold blue beneath the moon. Our holiday which had made this journey possible was by now almost over, but I was anxious that we should not end it without seeing the near-by zoo, which had a reputation as one of the best-kept in South America.

The zoo we had left behind in Buenos Aires was possibly South America's worst. Its animals were disease-ridden and starved, enclosed in tiny cages, or soaking in stagnant pools. When the military regime ended no one was really surprised by the announcement that the bones of some of the 'disappeared' had been found in the monkey compound. But the guidebook promised that this zoo, on the outskirts of

Mendoza, would be different. We drove through an avenue of poplars, back across the vineyards, and along a road that twisted its way above the city. At the top of a hill, known as the Cerro de la Gloria or the Ridge of Glory, there was a large monument to San Martín, the General who abandoned service in the Spanish army in 1812 and conducted a continental war of independence across Argentina, over the Andes to Chile and up the Pacific to Peru. There was not a town or village in Argentina that did not have a square, street or schoolroom named in his honour. But this was easily the biggest monument we had seen to this symbol of Argentina's ambition as a nation. It was no coincidence perhaps that this image of military prowess and conquest should stand over Mendoza, Argentina's last bastion of civilisation before the daunting barrier of the Andes and the perceived threat of Chile beyond. The statue was surmounted by a large bronze condor and the Goddess of Liberty. To one side some gates led into the zoo, which was set in a forest of eucalyptus and pine trees. Here visitors seemed to be more restricted by the narrowness of the path they had to follow than the animals were by their 'open' cages. But as we turned a corner, the balance changed, and it became clear that the animals were the prisoners. A group of monkeys were thrown together in a small compound. The tourists from Buenos Aires were laughing as the monkeys engaged in a vicious fight among themselves. Elsewhere, the condors and the llamas sat motionless on narrow rocks. Having come down from the mountains, they had lost all sense of purpose.

— 3 —

THE SHUTTLE TO
THE UPPERMOST LIMITS

It is very easy to do absolutely nothing at all on a Sunday in Buenos Aires. A sense of indolence pervades the city. But this Sunday we were more active than usual. We drove along the waterfront and went in search of history. Behind the sheet-metal huts of La Boca, the Italian quarter, there were rusty barges in the old port, dissected for scrap or sinking unceremoniously in the oily water. Near by, a child with mud on his face pulled a bell dedicated to William Brown, an Irish-born deserter from the British army who in the early nineteenth century had helped to 'liberate' the River Plate from the Spaniards. We walked along an unpaved alleyway, filled with pot-holes. There were failed artists touting their paintings and a hunchback feeding canaries in an iron house painted red and blue. There were walls lined with old men who went over their memories of the sea in a strange Italian dialect, and shouted obscenities at a prostitute as she gazed at them from behind a cracked windowpane. We followed a path where in the early nineteenth century, a regiment of English soldiers had been trapped by the people of Buenos Aires, throwing stones and barrels of burning oil.

Then we entered Plaza de Mayo, the city's centre where the pink palace of the presidency stood like a piece of marzipan. In front of it, a man in a monkey suit had climbed half-way up a flag-pole. The electronically controlled totem had blown a fuse and it had to be fixed before the next Day of the Army, so that the national colours could be raised on yet another day of homage to the armed forces. When we laughed, a policeman came to us and asked for our identity cards. 'You should have more respect,' he said, handing back our British passports. Across the square, a group of ceremonial guards dressed in top hats and breeches were marching towards the cathedral to guard the mausoleum of General José de San Martín, the nation's national hero. Policemen halted the traffic as they goose-stepped by. We ended up, not far from the closed Congress building, in the Café Tortoni listening to some tango. We had chocolate and fritters, encircled by mirrors and chandeliers, on marble tables where many years ago politicians had plotted over a game of chess. We planned our next journey, and decided we'd go south, to Patagonia, as far away as possible from sophistication and melancholy.

On the plane we sat next to Juan, a pale youth with an unformed beard who described himself as a war veteran. Juan didn't seem to mind that we were *Ingleses*; on the contrary it allowed him to let off steam. 'You know, my friend Pedro was blown up on the last day of the war. Now that's stupid, really stupid to get yourself killed like that, don't you think?'

Juan told me about his experiences with a mixture of bitterness and deep sadness. He remembered the officers who had given the orders but had not led their men, the crippling winter, the bad food. The terrifying professionalism of the English soldiers haunted him still. 'I have the same nightmares – *los Ingleses* coming with their bayonets, forgetting that we are not pillows but human beings like themselves. Stab and turn, stab and turn, that's what they learnt to do on the islands when things got bad.'

He told me about the English paratrooper who had looked after him as a prisoner of war. 'He said he admired the way we'd dealt with terrorism in Argentina and that with a few hundred "disappeared" in Ulster, the problem of the IRA would have been solved years ago.'

Juan stared at me through hollow eyes. 'You English, always think you are something special, eh? But in Ireland just like in South America you've always been *imperialistas*.'

'And what about the islands now that the Empire has won the war?' I asked.

Juan unwrapped his lunch tray, dissecting a cold chicken meticulously, before looking up stiffly and saying, 'The Malvinas have to be ours in the future. Otherwise what the fuck did we fight and die for?'

The plane flew us for about 2,500 kilometres over a land that rarely altered its tone or depth. This was midsummer in the southern hemisphere, and the herds of cattle that occasionally clustered on the prairie were like ants dug into a yellowish crust. Once the plane turned out towards the Atlantic and glided briefly over the seascape of undulating greys, only to return to the monotony of the dry country, larger than many nations but which Argentines like Juan, for all their nationalism, had always found difficult to populate.

The plane made a brief stopover in Río Gallegos, the capital of Santa Cruz province on the Patagonian coast. There, as we waited in our seats, the Argentine air force treated us to a display of their take-off skills. A squadron of Mirage jets appeared from behind some bunkers, looking like menacing eagles with their pointed noses and slits for windows. They moved down the runway, turned, and roared past us. 'Give us more of those, and we'd have won the war,' said Juan. These pilots too had been to the islands. But they had taken more of the glory than the conscripts. Now that the airport had been cleared of its infantry, the air force claimed to be the phoenix rising from the ashes of postwar Argentina.

Further south, we flew over some oil fields. When the first explorers had approached these parts from the Straits of Magellan, the bonfires which the local Indian tribes had burning on the shore had filled them with fear and wonder. But these blueish flames spouting from black towers were evidence only of the twentieth century, and the taming of Patagonia.

Soon we were landing at Río Grande, the last stop on our shuttle to Tierra del Fuego, South America's southernmost region. The guide-book described this Patagonian port as set in 'monotonous sheep-grazing plains', its only mark of distinction being that it was also the smallest and most southerly refinery in the world. It had little to offer the tourist, apart from an old Salesian mission eleven kilometres from the airport. But from the minute we stepped off the plane we were filled with apprehension. Just a few months before some colleagues of mine had been arrested here on unfounded spying charges. They had been taking photographs of the surrounding landscape and had British passports in their pockets. The memory played havoc with our sense of identity. At the customs barrier, a military policeman held a sub-machine-gun slung under his arm while he fingered through our passports. 'So you're *Ingleses?*' he asked with a tone of thinly veiled disgust. He stood under a poster of the Falkland Islands, declaring them Argentine. Juan walked past, saying 'Bye bye' with mocking familiarity. I felt trapped.

'Actually my father is Scottish, and my mother is Spanish, and I was born in Madrid. So I'm not really English at all,' I said, pronouncing my Castilian Spanish as best I could.

'And what about her?' he said, looking up for the first time to look at Kidge. His face was heavily boned and his eyes, like Juan's, seemed to have been drained of life. 'My family's from Ireland originally,'

Kidge said. The policeman said Ireland was part of the United Kingdom and that is why the English sent troops there. At that moment, in my paranoia, I suspected that my conversation with Juan had been relayed in advance of our arrival. I could envisage a nightmare sequence, beginning with our arrest, and ending, like my colleagues, in some damp cell in Tierra del Fuego, separated for months, if not years.

Even after the policeman had handed back our passport and told us we could move on, I saw him confer with a man in a blue suit and a thick beard who I had no doubt belonged to the security forces. I felt that every move we made, however innocently motivated, only incriminated us further. The airport seemed like a small room filled with staring eyes. It was not hard to imagine that if we stayed in the airport for the whole two hours of the stopover something terrible would happen. We walked outside and stood at a bus stop, and self-consciously began to look at our tourist guide. Then a naval Captain dressed in khaki uniform got out of his car, and walked towards us. I asked him the way to the Salesian mission. He said he was just stopping off at the airport to pick up some mail, but he offered to give us a lift for most of the way. I watched him go into the airport lounge, fearful that he would talk to the policeman and the man with the beard. But I could not see them any more, and when the Captain re-emerged, his unsuspecting attitude towards us seemed unchanged.

So the three of us drove off. Kidge, in the back seat, was pretending to be asleep so she would not have to engage in conversation. I, with my Castilian accent again, told tales of being a Spanish tourist in Argentina. The officer had greased-backed hair and a moustache neatly trimmed over his upper lip. He looked at himself in the side mirror, then offered me a cigarette and turned on the radio. It was playing a Beatles song. He switched it off. 'So you're a *madrileño*. My grandparents were Italian . . . Oh Patagonia, there's some excellent trout fishing, but you know it's not beautiful like parts of Europe.'

Looking out at the landscape that surrounded us, it was hard not to agree with him. As far as the eye could see, Patagonia – or at least this part of Patagonia – was a semi-desert of dust and clumps of wild weed. Here and there square-shaped concrete bungalows stood out as a token human presence in the midst of so much emptiness. It looked like Castile in August, but without the villages.

The officer drove us along a fence covered with Danger – Keep Out signs. One sign declared the area the exclusive preserve of the

Argentine navy. I asked him if this was the Salesian mission. He laughed and then must have noticed the strain in my face for he said, 'Don't look so worried . . . I just want to see if I've got any messages.' He left us by the gates of the naval base, sitting in his car. He had switched the radio on again and this time there was someone singing 'Cambalache', one of the most popular of all Argentine tango songs.

The singer was lamenting that nothing ever changed in Argentina, whether you were good, bad, or plain stupid. This was not the tango 'for export' to Parisian night clubs, or New York cabarets. Nor was it the tango of operatic machos and their shattered love lives. It was the tango of subversion that Argentines liked to listen to whenever they felt that a change of regime was in the air. I could see small contingents of ragged conscripts in fatigues marching with some bugles, and a line of Super Etendards, the French-made planes which carry the Exocet missiles. As Kidge emerged from her 'sleep', the paranoia we had shared at the airport returned.

'I wish I hadn't seen anything,' Kidge said, looking at the military base from the corner of her eye. For a moment we felt sure that the Captain had gone to ring up the airport to check us out.

'No messages,' the Captain said when he came back to the car.

'Cambalache' was still putting over the same message. The Captain switched the radio off. He was carrying some books and cans of beer, one of which he offered to me. He drove us for about two more miles, telling me about all the TV sets and the record players Japanese companies were manufacturing in the area. 'The land's not worth a peso. But no one pays taxes and the labour's cheap so who complains?' The Captain's expressions echoed those of the tango. They were measured to the point of exaggeration, for maximum theatrical effect. I was relieved when he finally said he had to get home and dropped us at the next crossroads.

The man who gave us a lift the rest of the way was a Chilean truck driver, called Augusto – 'I was named after my uncle, not after Pinochet,' he said, his large body suddenly convulsed in laughter. He had a blue handkerchief tied round his head and a picture of the Pope hanging from his mirror. He had no teeth at all and since he was driving a very old truck we had to shout in order to hear each other above the din of the engine.

The road now turned into a rough track running parallel with the beach. The sand was filled with trenches and gun emplacements which had been dug during a false alarm about a Chilean invasion several years before. There was no one about except for a flock of seagulls that delicately paddled where the waves traced the shoreline. I told Augusto about all the industrial development the Captain had boasted of and he let out another loud chuckle. 'Development here?' he shouted. 'This part of the country would be totally depopulated if it wasn't for us Chileans. The man from Buenos Aires makes as much money as he can in as short a time as possible and then he goes away. It's the Chileans who stay.'

Augusto reminded me that successive Argentine governments had shown a great deal of duplicity in their dealings with the Chileans, in much the same way as the English had done with their immigrant labour. At the beginning they had been taken in as necessary participants in the region's development. But then, when the economy had slipped into crisis and the military had begun their war games, the Chileans had been relegated to the status of third-class citizens, and classified as a security risk. Whenever tension rose on the Chilean–Argentine border, the Argentine government ordered mass deportations. 'The junta is worse than our Pinochet,' shouted Augusto.

It was as I listened to Augusto, that I began to suspect there was nothing romantic about Patagonia any more. In the 1960s when it was hip to think about how to survive a nuclear war, this part of the world, for all its starkness, became the ultimate fallout shelter, where with a bit of luck the bomb would never reach you. Elsewhere there could be whole cities turned to rubble and countryside laid waste by clouds filled with radioactive rain. But to be in Patagonia was to join Butch Cassidy, the Welsh and the rabbits, near the furthermost limits of the earth, untouched and untouchable. The Falklands War changed all that, at least anything that hadn't changed already with the passing of the hippies. It was from here that the Argentines had planned and executed their attacks on the British Task Force; it was to here that the wounded and the dead were brought back. Río Gallegos and Río Grande ceased to be dusty frontiers, towns of interest only to extroverts or train buffs. They became transit lounges for shrouded coffins.

In a sense, the Falklands experience and the 'dirty war' of 'disappearances' which preceded it under the junta were rather more consistent with Patagonia's underlying history than the hippies. The region's identity was defined long before contemporary warfare, let alone the atom bomb, was invented. The Argentine nation was not born with General San Martín and the nineteenth-century War of Independence from Spain but as a result of subsequent plunder. Patagonia's early inhabitants were nomadic Indians who lived by hunting across a vast area that is today southern Argentina and southern Chile. The Onas, Yaghans, Tehuelcans – as the early tribes were called – had more in common with the Red Indians of the south-western United States and the Mongolians of Asia than with the Inca and Aztec civilisations – although exactly when and how the demographic split took place remains a mystery. In Patagonia, survival of the fittest began with the hunt up river for otters and seals, in small inlets and coves for fish and mussels, and on the vast expanse of land for the guanaco. This elegant, effeminate first cousin of the llama provided food and clothing for the Indians. Across the wild land, the guanaco only defended itself by running, and, once surrounded by the hunters, usually froze in confused terror.

Then came the white man. First the missionaries, next the gold prospectors, and finally the sheep farmers and the military. In an old settlement called Wulaia, the missions found the Indians' instinct was much the same as it had been for about two thousand years. One day in November 1859, a small group of Anglican missionaries led by the Reverend Garland Philips put ashore near some wigwams and enthusiastically, Bibles in hand, set about erecting their own huts. One bright and clear Sunday morning, the mission was complete. It was a moment all missionaries dreamed about: savagery alongside civilisation, one gaping at the other, apparently ready to accept and convert to it, the devil on bended knee and God supreme. But the celebration hymn never got further than the first line. First, flying through the air, came the spears, the arrows and the stones. Then the Indians arrived and tore the white men to bits. Alfred Cole, the mission's cook, survived. He was left to tell the tale after the Indians had plucked his beard and eyebrows and stripped him of his clothes. Such examples of Indian practice were engrained in the white settlers' consciousness and in subsequent years plunder was answered with plunder.

As in other parts of the New World, the Indians were decimated by alien disease and firepower. In 1884, Colonel Augusto Lasserre led an expedition from Buenos Aires to claim the most southerly region of Tierra del Fuego for the Argentine Republic. Down went the missionaries' flag, up went the Argentine blue and white; there was a salvo of twenty-one guns, and Lasserre gave the local settlers full rights to the land. The Colonel, however, had overlooked the fact that his small army of adventurers was riddled with measles. Their germs spread through the settlement and beyond, and soon the missionaries couldn't dig graves fast enough.

After Lasserre came General Roca, at the head of Argentina's first 'national' army. The government in Buenos Aires decreed that the southern provinces should be civilised irreversibly, and the army took it upon itself to end once and for all the threat posed by the Indians. Roca's campaign has gone down in Argentine history books as a heroic feat, comparable to General San Martín's crossing of the Andes. In fact, the 'Conquest of the Desert' was genocide. Argentines who today proudly proclaim their country as the only one in the Third World without a colour problem thank Roca for wiping out large sectors of the Indian race. Far less space is given in Argentine history books to the Salesian order, the Catholic missionaries who did what they could to save the Indians from extinction. But thanks to Augusto, our truck driver, we were able to find some of the remnants of a plundered race.

As we approached, a faint smell of cooked cabbage was coming from the Salesian school. The construction of roughly painted wood and corrugated iron was rattling in the wind. Padre Francisco, the rector, stood in the main doorway. He was unshaven, fat and dressed in a white frock that hung about him loosely. He had a wrinkled face but I suspected that the weather rather than hard work had chiselled him. By contrast, the small boy who stood beside him had the haunted looks and physical dislocation of a stray dog. He had very dark eyes and a jagged fringe of black hair and was scratching his right knee with a hand that seemed to have not an ounce of fat on it. He was introduced by Padre Francisco as Diego, 'my favourite pupil'. There were 139 boys like him in the mission, who had been delivered to the holy fathers by the local community.

'There's not much money coming in from the government. In fact I think I'd close the place down were it not for the kindness of the local *estancieros*,' said Padre Francisco.

'But what do the boys do here?' I asked. Diego was showing the first signs of being bored with our conversation and was scratching with greater intent.

'Oh, the boys . . . well, they're learning agriculture,' said Padre Francisco.

In Argentina, an *estanciero* is someone who owns a large farm, and in Patagonia families with Spanish- and English-sounding names own farms the size of small English counties thanks to the 'Conquest of the Desert'. When people like Padre Francisco talk of boys such as Diego learning about agriculture, you know that the lesson is similar to a course in Latin or Greek: it has only indirect use in later life. For those who learn about agriculture will not grow up to own *estancias*. At best they will be small farmers, although, more likely, they will work on the *estancia*.

Padre Francisco said he had some business to attend to and left us alone with Diego. When Kidge took him by the hand, he stopped scratching and spoke for the first time. 'Come, I'll show you the museum.' The museum was housed in what used to be the old mission church. Its doors creaked, and the first room we walked into had no light. Diego led us up a narrow staircase to a room filled with old studio photographs of Indians. They looked stiff and self-conscious. They were pictured clutching bows and spears and covered in their guanaco skins. Their immobility and subjection before the camera was an image of final surrender. In an adjoining room, there were some glass show-cases containing bows and spears, and two commemorative plates recording the efforts of nineteenth-century engineers from Liverpool and Lincolnshire. There was no hispanic grafting here – simply a clear divide between Indian Patagonia and industrial, imperialist Britain. For, thanks to General Roca, the British had built the railroads.

The shuttle completed its journey somewhat shakily after encountering turbulence between the black mountains of Tierra del Fuego. As we cleared the cloud, it dipped down over dense pine forest and flew in a half circle across the green waters of the Beagle Channel. The shoreline was shrouded in dark mist. On catching sight of this island in the extreme south of South America for the first time in 1832, Charles Darwin had described it as the 'cursed land'. We were touched with a sense of melancholy.

The island's only town, Ushuaia, was filled with soldiers. Most of them seemed to have little to do except wander down the main street, whose duty-free shops were filled with everything from electric toothbrushes to videos. The civilian population was tucked away in offices or in small houses perched on a ridge overlooking the harbour. The houses had crooked wooden verandas and sheet-metal roofs and most of their front gardens were overgrown with weeds.

Argentines like to think of Ushuaia as a sister town to Port Stanley, the capital of the Falklands, which lies just a couple of hours' flying time away. In 1980 Tierra del Fuego was close to becoming the

Falklands' main trading partner – an idea which might have altered the course of history had it been allowed to develop. The *fueginos* wanted to export their wood and Japanese-made appliances. The kelpers wanted to get rid of some surplus sheep for re-export from Argentina or for use in Tierra del Fuego as bait for the local crab industry. One person who had seen the possibilities was Natalie Goodall. She had led a Fuegian mission to the Falklands, only to have her hopes of reconciliation dashed by the attitudes of some of the more intransigent local inhabitants. Natalie was an expatriate American naturalist married to an Englishman. I was anxious to see her because I had been told she was one of the few people who was doing something in Ushuaia. She seemed to be a person more interested in what she had to say than in the way she looked – in contrast with the officers I had seen swaggering down the main street. She was very large and dressed in loose-fitting trousers and t-shirt. She treated us suspiciously at first, all the more so in response to my claim that I had been given her name by a British diplomat in Buenos Aires. 'I'm not English, you know, it's my husband who is English,' she said, blocking the doorway to her small house a few yards along from the harbour.

Eventually she took us down some stairs to what she called her 'work place' – a cramped basement studio filled with fish scales and stuffed sharks. The air was thick with the smell of rotting fish. The room was poorly lit and in one corner, barely illuminated by a small desk lamp, sat a young, rather pretty blonde girl whom Natalie introduced as her daughter. 'This is where I escape to and write about the natural history of Tierra del Fuego,' Natalie said. When I asked her if she had ever thought of writing a history of the Falklands, she said she preferred to put behind her a tale of conflicting loyalties and tragedy. During the Falklands War, she had contributed to the junta's Patriotic Fund by auctioning reproductions of her paintings of the Fuegian landscape and an early book she had written on the area. She had also joined the local choir, who had sung to the crew of the battle cruiser *Belgrano* before it had set sail. 'You see I believe the Malvinas really do belong to Argentina,' she said.

'But where's the conflict?' I asked.

'My English husband,' she said with a look of long-standing suffering. She then told me that she had been one of the few local people who had gone to the near-by military jail to visit the three British journalists arrested on spying charges. She had taken them books and talked to them in English, for which they were doubly thankful. 'A

few days after this, it was Argentina's national day. The local population took to the streets shouting anti-British slogans and waving
their flags. I suddenly found it all excessive and decided, for reasons
of health, to stop singing for the troops.'

Nevertheless Natalie told me how on the night before the *Belgrano*
had left for the Falklands, she had taken her teenage daughter to a
party at the local military barracks given for the departing conscript
sailors and the local population. 'Everyone was dancing and singing,
having a great time, as if it was the end of a school term or a marriage
feast,' Natalie recalled. The dancing partner of the daughter, who sat
with us, was now somewhere at the bottom of the South Atlantic, if
he had not already been eaten by the fish. I asked the daughter what
she felt. 'I am and always will be Argentine,' she snapped. Then she
got up and left.

And yet her father was British, Thomas Goodall, the great-grandson
of Thomas Bridges. Natalie told me about her uncle-in-law, Adrian,
who ran an *estancia* just south of Río Grande. 'He's very pro-Argentine
just like me. During the war he helped the navy by translating intercepted messages from the Task Force.'

'Conflicting loyalties, again, I suppose,' I ventured.

'Yes, I guess you could say that,' Natalie said. I looked around the
'work-room'. The atmosphere was very close now, almost sub-aquatic,
with the stuffed sharks glowering menacingly. Natalie had talked
about the sinking of the *Belgrano* and about treason redefined as
loyalty and about almost every other member of the family. 'What
about Tom?' I asked.

'He doesn't live here. He lives out on the camp. You'll find it very
difficult to find him.' So we went in search of Tom Goodall.

In 1851 the Reverend George Pakenham Despard, BA, pastor of
Lenton, Nottinghamshire, found a baby boy. He had been abandoned
on a small footbridge in Bristol. There were no messages or documents
on the child, but he was dressed in an immaculate frock and around
his neck was a locket engraved with the letter 'T'. The Reverend
Despard decided that the child was Catholic and from a rich family
and adopted him. He christened him Thomas. The boy was eventually
told the circumstances of his adoption and chose for himself the
surname Bridges in memory of the meeting that had saved his life.
Thomas grew up to be a clergyman like his adopted father and founded
the Patagonian Missionary Society in Tierra del Fuego.

The story of Thomas was outlined to us by his only surviving granddaughter, Clarita, over tea and scones in the midst of a large farming estate behind the mountains of Ushuaia. To get there I had driven along a winding road lined with pines, boulders and running streams but not a trace of humanity. Then the tarmac had turned to dirt track running through a seemingly limitless expanse of rolling prairie covered in coarse grass and petrified trees. There were thousands of sheep grazing across the country, like specks of cotton floating on a huge ocean of turbulent green water. This was Port Harberton, the 50,000 acre *estancia* granted to the Reverend Bridges and his descendants by General Roca.

In his autobiography, Lucas Bridges, son of Thomas, describes General Roca as an 'enlightened and progressive statesman who, in his day, had led more than one punitive expedition against the turbulent *pampa* Indians . . . he had done more than any of his contemporaries to bring those fierce tribes to order.' The Reverend Bridges comes through the pages of the book as a courageous and humane missionary who held in disdain Darwin's culturally selective description of the Indian inhabitants of Tierra del Fuego as 'cannibals' and the 'missing link'. Bridges treated the Indians in his settlement with understanding and love, yet his collaboration with Roca was to be echoed by subsequent generations. Many years later, when the military coup of 1976 led to the abduction, torture and disappearance of over 9,000 Argentines, the Anglo-Argentine community likewise retreated behind the boundaries of their properties and turned a blind eye to the horrors taking place beyond their manicured lawns. Their lifestyle was unaffected by the actions of the junta; if anything it was secured as the death squads led their punitive expeditions against turbulent political dissidents and did more than any of their contemporaries to bring those 'fierce tribes' to order. Only with the outbreak of the Falklands War, once their own world was threatened for the first time, did the loyalties of the Anglo-Argentines come under strain.

Clarita was quite unlike any Anglo-Argentine I had met in Buenos Aires. She owed no one any favours, had no need to concede. There was no pretence about her, no trying to speak Spanish with an English accent or English with the token Spanish word. After all these years she was beyond good or evil, knowing that she would have to leave the world as she had entered it, English to the bone. She looked younger than her ninety years. Her white hair was neatly collected in a bun; her light green eyes quite alert; I felt she would have not looked out of place pushing a pram in Kensington Gardens.

Her home was unchanged from the day Bridges had built it out of timber brought from England and local wood in 1887. In the spot where I stood, with the land sloping upwards behind it to the north-east, the homestead received the benefit of the summer sun till well on in the afternoon. Bridges' son had written, 'Then the sheltering hill at the back cast its heavy shadows over the place, and the hills and the woods across the harbour would stand out with marvellous clearness as daylight faded. This was the hour when father and mother, arm in arm, would take their evening stroll, until the dusk crept over the land and the air grew chilly. Then it was that the reflection of the hills on the calm, darkening water made a picture of peace beyond my power to describe.'

We had arrived at Harberton about teatime after driving along the lake that marks its eastern border, and that picture of peace had in no sense been diluted by the passage of time. We sat in Clarita's 'parlour', sharing her selection of jams, letting the tea brew in the tea pot, passing the scones round reverentially. 'I'm afraid I've had to make them with margarine. They've run out of butter down in Ushuaia,' she said. Then an officer from the local naval base arrived uninvited. 'Oh, it's dear Captain Galines, he's come on what he so charmingly describes as a courtesy call,' said Clarita, steadily pouring herself another cup of tea.

Captain Galines was a handsome young man. Blond, blue-eyed and trim in his khaki fatigues. I was struck by his hands. They were immaculate. He spoke English with an Oxford accent and before sitting down asked 'Lady Clara' for permission to take his pistol holster off and hang it on a chair. I wondered if he had ever gaped at a woman prisoner having an electric prod pressed up into her vagina.

'What a coincidence you've come, Captain,' said Clarita passing him the scones. 'My friend from Buenos Aires and I were just saying what a good thing this Falklands business is over. I still can't under-stand why your colleagues wasted so much time over it. It all seemed so very silly.'

Galines looked at me and smiled, nodded his head from side to side and then up and down, and wiped the crumbs of a scone from the tablecloth. He then cleared his throat, and raising himself slightly in his chair said, 'My dear Lady Clarita, you know that if I agreed with you I would not with pride and honour be wearing this uniform. *Las*

Malvinas son Argentinas, were, are, and always will be. But I am a reasonable man so I will say this: the kelpers will never want to be Argentine until we can provide a good government, one that is stable and trustworthy. I know that we, the military, could have provided that if your Mrs Thatcher hadn't sent her Task Force. We do, after all, believe in Christian values as strongly as the Reverend Bridges himself . . . '

Galines went on talking for a long time. Clarita, after her initial intervention, appeared to float off into a daydream and I was far too cowed even to attempt an argument. When I came to write the notes for my diary, I left out the main text of his speech, for everything he had to say about the war and the disappeared was mere repetition of a thousand military communiqués of the kind I had sought escape from on this journey. But finally Galines came to a conclusion and Clarita returned, briefly, to earth. Galines asked me, 'Well, it seems I have done most of the talking . . . tell me, sir, what brings you to Tierra del Fuego?'

Before I had even thought of an answer, Clarita said, 'He's a journalist, dear, he's come to write all about us.'

Galines gave an empty laugh, strapped on his pistol and made as if to leave. At the door, he kissed Clarita's hand and turning towards me said, 'We have to be careful with journalists, they are usually spies.' He then bid us goodbye and left.

Later, as the dusk was creeping over the land and we were walking along Clarita's rose-filled garden border, Tom, her son and the husband of Natalie, arrived. In his dungarees and Wellington boots, he looked identical to the bearded young man with dark, penetrating eyes who stared out from the pages of Lucas Bridges' autobiography. Tom acknowledged his mother with a grunt, glanced at us suspiciously, and, when he was told he had just missed Galines, mumbled, 'Not that bastard again . . . ' before disappearing into the house. Only afterwards, when the four of us sat by the log fire in the sitting room, did he relax his lanky frame in an armchair, and light a pipe. Outside, the buildings had begun to rattle and whistle in the driving wind and the day had entered the lengthy twilight of a January evening in the southernmost region of the world. The room closed about us with its warmth and comfort. It was filled with books – again untouched from the first days of Bridges – volumes of Dickens, the *Leisure Hour* and *Sunday at Home*. Clarita looked at Kidge's face glowing by the fireside. 'You really are an English rose, my dear,' Clarita said before going into one of her waking sleeps again. Tom, drawing hard and long at his pipe and looking steadily at the fire, said, 'Forget the crap Galines gave you. The kelpers look after their gardens and have an administration that works. Look at Ushuaia, everything's in a mess. The governor has over 1,000 civil servants and the biggest concentrated military presence in South America and yet he can't even cook a fried egg.'

He had no illusions about what might have happened to the kelpers had the Argentine armed forces been allowed to stay on the islands. He had his own experience to measure a hypothetical guess by. Just before Christmas 1978, when General Leopoldo Galtieri, then army chief, decided that Chile was planning to invade Patagonia, the Argentine armed forces declared Port Harberton a potential battle-field. Without waiting for his permission or offering any kind of compensation, Galtieri's soldiers drove their jeeps across the fields of the Bridges' estate, breaking down the fences and ploughing through the herds of sheep along the way. The 'strategic' southern route the military carved out of the fields – a dirt track from the mountains to the sea – killed off about 500 sheep. During the Falklands War, while his brother Adrian intercepted British messages, his wife Natalie sang to the Argentine troops and his daughters fell in love with the conscripts, Tom was put under virtual house arrest. Now, six months after the war had ended, he was going on trial for transporting his Chilean farmhands across the border without the necessary papers. As we shared a bottle of whisky and watched the flames dancing, Tom told me he had just come from Ushuaia where he had been organising his defence. 'If they fine me, I'll prosecute them for killing my sheep,' he said.

Tierra del Fuego was a hot-bed of Argentine nationalism where passions had grown more extreme as a result of the Falklands War. But it still owed much of its discovery, settlement and conversion to Western civilisation to the British. Therein lies the historical irony. Before the Reverend Bridges there were other missionaries, and before them captains of the Royal Navy, adventurers and pirates, whose very English names were immortalised on the Fuegian map. Nevertheless the Argentines are not entirely unjustified in blaming some of their conflicts on the British. It was the confused and ambiguous charting of the waters and small islands in the Beagle Channel in the early nineteenth century by Captain Robert Fitzroy that gave the Argentines and the Chileans an ongoing territorial dispute for over one hundred years. A treaty signed in 1881 by Argentina and Chile, under the auspices of Britain, aspired to define the area in litigation. To the Argentine Republic went Staten Island, the small islands next to it, and the other islands 'there may be on the Atlantic to the east of Tierra del Fuego and off the eastern coast of Patagonia'. To Chile went 'all the islands to the south of the Beagle Channel up to Cape Horn and those there may be to the west of Tierra del Fuego'. Fitzroy never quite defined where the Beagle Channel began and where it ended, and in 1881 Argentina and Chile had signed a peace treaty open to a wealth of interpretations. It was a recipe for disaster which had already brought the two countries to the brink of war on at least two occasions in the twentieth century.

In that January of 1983, we glimpsed a sense of territorial confusion on board an Argentine pleasure cruiser called the *Ángel B*. We boarded in Ushuaia harbour, about twenty yards away from where the *Belgrano* had docked for the last time. The other passengers were all members of a package tour from Buenos Aires. They tumbled on board early one morning, jewelled, scented and wrapped in furs, as if in readiness not for a short channel hop in a rundown steam ferry but for a transatlantic luxury cruise aboard the *QE2*. As the *Ángel B* steamed slowly out of the harbour, a group of Upland geese, which had been floating on the water, scattered in panic. There was a quick burst of the Argentine national anthem out of one of the loudspeakers in the boat, and then Rodolfo, our guide, began his commentary. 'On our right, we have Navarin Island. It belongs to the republic of Chile and there is now a naval base there – Puerto Williams. This is the southernmost port in the world, but – please note – it is not, repeat not, the southernmost city in the world – Ushuaia is of course the southernmost city in the world and it is ARGENTINO.'

An old woman was not convinced. She had heard somewhere that Navarin was Argentine and now began to sing the national anthem. 'Oh, hear the mortal cry, liberty, liberty, liberty,' she sang. Below deck, the other passengers seemed oblivious to her performance. They talked about politics in Buenos Aires, inflation and the price of a colour TV, and all the while the Beagle Channel slipped by like a piece of unwanted sewage. Only a German couple stood it out on deck. The woman took photographs while the man filmed methodically. Around us the mountains had turned grey and metallic under the morning light and the water was agitated and spotted with their reflections.

In more tempestuous times than these, Chilean and Argentine naval boats had grown accustomed to firing at each other as an assertion of their sovereignty rights. Tradition has it that sailors on deck would also pull their trousers down and turn their backs whenever the enemy came within range. It was more like a game than a war. As we steamed along, I couldn't help reflecting for a moment on the *Belgrano*'s last voyage. Some of the sailors would have been below deck, but others would have been above, like myself and the German couple, looking out at the black mountains and the albatross gliding like a bad omen across the green waters.

The *Ángel B* reached the high point of its two-hour cruise: a moss-covered piece of floating rock called the Isla de los Lobos. My fellow passengers struggled reluctantly on deck only to be confronted by the most appalling smell – a mixture of rotting seaweed, shit and urine. The loudspeakers once again crackled into action as Rodolfo tried to focus eyes rather than noses. 'You will now see the sealions – and you will notice they like showing off, that's why they are turning their bottoms at you.' The old woman who had previously sung the national anthem buried her face in her muffler, and pressed her hands deep into her pockets in an apparent attempt to avoid all skin contact with the air. Her husband stumbled after her, making jokes. 'Someone round here has not had a bath,' he said. The other passengers looked embarrassedly at each other, and then the jokes came in thick and fast, all about smells. It was a scatological catharsis which for a moment brought a scene of contrived good humour to the *Ángel B*. I was reminded of what an Argentine friend had once said about the people of Buenos Aires – they love showing you their sitting rooms, but they will try and rush you past their bathrooms.

Meanwhile, below us on the rock, some twenty sealions and sea elephants were sleeping slothfully or else moving with difficulty. The lions had copper-coloured bodies with golden manes. The elephants were greyish white and, without the two back flippers of the lions, could only move with a forward ripple of the body. Gerald Durrell, in his book on South American wildlife, describes sealions as 'expert lions, exercising restraint and rhythm and an example to mankind'. I searched for inspiration. But the image that stuck was that of obese old men dressed in mustard-coloured t-shirts, taking the sun.

Lucas Bridges described 1885 as 'momentous'. It was the year that Captain Félix Paz of the Argentine navy was appointed first military governor of Tierra del Fuego. Paz got on handsomely with the Bridges family. He gave Thomas Bridges a horse, a 'chestnut with a distinguished Roman nose', and took his boys out on frequent canoeing expeditions around the islands. Thus, when Natalie Goodall volunteered to introduce me to Tierra del Fuego's current governor, Admiral Suárez del Cerro, I felt it was an opportunity I couldn't miss. One hundred years after Paz, the governorship of Tierra del Fuego had expanded to encompass the Antarctic and the 'islands in the South Atlantic'; such claims were not based on occupation but on the assumption that a territory could be annexed merely by stating that it was. Del Cerro's main claim to fame was to have been one of the men originally considered by General Galtieri to act as the first administrator of the Malvinas after the 2 April invasion. Such a post would have given the navy effective control over the whole operation. But Galtieri, an army man, wanted to go down in history, so he had given the job to General Menéndez instead. Del Cerro was given Ushuaia as compensation. There he had gained a reputation for skilfully managed corruption, using the governor's approval of planning applications as a form of lucrative patronage, and the town's twin-engined hospital plane for his own personal travel to and from Buenos Aires.

The governor had his headquarters in a large office block which dwarfed most of the buildings in Ushuaia. Within it hundreds of local Civil Servants worked on the governor's personal affairs, for in Tierra del Fugeo there were few taxes to collect. The Admiral's rooms were at the end of a long corridor filled with the noise of machines of one sort or another, and smelling vaguely of detergent. Del Cerro was sitting enthroned behind a huge desk, like the chairman of the board. He was dressed in a dark pinstriped suit and was dictating a letter to a secretary. He stopped as soon as I walked in, and brusquely dismissed her. He told me that the audience could only last five minutes as he had some urgent personal business to attend to. He then turned and pointed to a map behind his desk which had most of the south Atlantic, including the Falklands and the Antarctic coloured in the blue and white of the national flag. There followed the official text of the junta's case on the Malvinas which I had heard so often in Buenos Aires. I took no notes, but I remember that he ended with this comment, 'Sooner or later the islands will be back in Argentine hands, either through diplomacy or force. I hope it will eventually be through diplomacy because you English will realise it's not worth the cost.'

Also I recall that I reminded him about the chestnut with the Roman nose which the former governor had given Lucas Bridges. 'Maybe if we traded horses again and dropped this sovereignty business, we might be friends,' I said. But the Admiral had no horses to give away other than those General Galtieri had sent to Colonel Qadafi in thanks for the arms Libya had sent during the war. In Ushuaia, there was money to be made in tax forms and real estate and Tom Goodall was facing trial. Now the Admiral was cutting short our conversation because he had a plane to catch.

Other travellers had ended their voyage to South America in Ushuaia. But I knew that for us to do that would be a form of dying. What we had found in that soulless town was barely the beginning. There was nothing there but attitudes we had grown accustomed to in Buenos Aires, which had been grafted on, redefined and emphasised, and which left me with an even greater longing for escape. We looked for a bus that would take us anywhere in Tierra del Fuego except Ushuaia. It led us to a lake, where we took a boat to Perrito Moreno, site of one of the world's oldest glaciers. On the shoreline, at the foot of the black hills, we waited for the boat on a beach backed by a wood of beech trees and wild flowers. There were anemones and yellow violets, buttercups, clover and dandelion scattered across a field of lush grass – the warmth of the pastoral setting seemed a world removed from the ghostlike atmosphere of much of Tierra del Fuego.

The boat steamed over milky waters, where we were soon encountering one of the most dramatic scenes we had yet seen in South America. Across the lake the icebergs began to appear. The younger ones, formed only recently, were porous and full of air bubbles and were clustered together in powdery lumps. The oldest ones, more than a thousand years old, were sharp angled and transparent, and stuck out from the water like cracked glass. Then there were the most beautiful bergs of them all, with their futuristic shapes of azure marble blending at the waterline into the deepest blue. I was as comforted by this remnant of the Ice Age as I had been by the wild flowers, secure in the knowledge that nature had a life of its own, separate from Admiral del Cerro. At the furthest corner of the lake, a snow field had formed above the valley and was divided by ridges covered in forest. The lowest portions of the glacier were amassed in thick contours of snow on the edge of the lake. They trembled in the sun in a contorted dance like sheeted ghosts. Perched on a hill overlooking the lake sat hundreds of people in strange hats, looking through field glasses and telescopes, or propped up behind cameras placed on tripods. They reminded me of pilgrims waiting for an apparition. One of the boat's sailors told Kidge that many of these people were tourists, but that some were fanatical naturalists who had been waiting there for three months with little food, water or sleep, so as not to miss a moment of rare geological evolution: when the pressure from the higher fields of ice eroded and broke through the lakeside barrier. Moreno was famed as the only glacier left in the world that was still 'advancing'. For many hours we sat with them watching as, periodically, chunks of ice broke off and crashed into the lake, raising the level of the water and provoking small tidal waves as the thunderclaps reverberated across the mountains. Here, where the waste of ice had proved greater than the supply, the glacier was scientifically deemed to have ended. But I knew it wasn't so and sat watching a process as cyclical as life itself. Supply and demand varied according to the level of snowfall or the heat of the summer, or the timing of a nuclear test. I had read that glaciers had a cycle of contraction and expansion about every fifty years. Perrito Moreno was due for a massive birth that year.

We caught another bus. It was empty except for two couples from Buenos Aires. One of the women despaired of the lack of Indians as she sat chewing on packets of cheese biscuits. 'I expected this to be like the Wild West with the tribes riding bare-backed and throwing spears,' said one of them. 'I told you we should have gone to Miami instead,' said her husband. The plains of Patagonia spread out monotonously. Only once on that journey did movement impose itself on the desolation. We passed a pair of wild ostriches who fled once the bus had covered them in dust. They had huge eyelashes and upturned noses and bottoms that seemed to be covered by crêpe paper. They rustled as they skipped off in the direction of Perrito Moreno.

For two hours the bus rattled and bumped its way along the rustic highway until a mountain called Fitzroy came into view. It had jagged contours of black granite reaching out of the clouds, seemingly from this world but not of it. Long ago the Araucanian Indian tribes that roamed Patagonia thought of this mountain as a god. It was venerated as the centre of their mythology. They called it Chalten, which means 'god of smoke'. The Indians would watch the strange ring of clouds that form around the mountain peak at sunset and believe that this was a sacred breath coming from deep within an all-powerful spirit. Because they respected Chalten, they never sought to conquer it.

We stayed that night at the base of the mountain in a wooden lodge that had been converted into a hotel. It had a large sitting room filled with tourist posters, advertisements for climbing equipment and photographs of climbers of every nationality who had scaled the mountain's steep face and reached the summit. Mónica Vázquez, the proprietor, ran the hotel like a barracks, insisting that we should all eat and go to bed at the same time and that there should be silence after ten o'clock. 'The English climbers came in 1980. They haven't come back since. I think they would be unwise to do so,' Mónica told me. That night, we walked into our room to find that someone had put a printed sheet of paper on the bedside table. It said, 'Dear resident, welcome to Fitzroy, a piece of Argentine soil. We want you to enjoy your stay but do not forget where you are. Feel proud that this is Argentina, and you will help us assert our sovereignty.' I looked out of the window. There was a yellowish half-moon, bordered by clouds, perched on the edge of the mountain. I fell asleep in Kidge's arms, thinking that in the days of Chalten, long before Mónica Vázquez existed, there were no flags. Only Indians who looked up at the huge mountain face, thinking of it as doubly great – a source of infinite threat and a protection. The mountain did not separate the world, but was the world. Now the mountain, renamed after an Englishman, was claimed by Argentina and Chile. But Chalten belonged to an age when maps had not been drawn.

— 4 —

LOOKING FOR DONA FLOR

Behind the Casa Rosada, the newspapers report, they have excavated a customs house filled with ghosts, not of damp chambers and electrified beds, but of Spanish merchants with clean coats. And yet it is there that we watched the Madres trampled by police horses, and Juan Pérez shot in the heart. Outside the presidential palace, the Ford Falcons have number plates and a new polish, and the graffiti is fading . . . Don't let me forget the tear caught in the white bandanna and the looks of indifference and hate behind the riot shields. For I am afraid of the reflection of your faces or the transparency of looking forward.

'You can tell we are in France, *che*,' said Alejandro Puenzo to Leandro Morandini one July morning in 1983. The two friends from childhood, now junior managers in one of Argentina's less reputable financial institutions, had begun their family holiday. Not in France, which was still 10,000 kilometres away, but on a skyborne French colony – the Air France Jumbo from Buenos Aires to Paris via Rio de Janeiro.

The plane had risen slowly over the River Plate and was now cruising over Uruguay. Supper was being served. Alejandro was helping himself from a bottle of champagne. When he and Leandro had drunk it, he asked for another one. 'Yes, you can tell we are in France, *che*,' said Leandro. They were both quite drunk now and barely took notice of the bill that had landed on their dinner trays. They were transfixed by the body of the air hostess as she walked away from them down the gangway. 'Just look at that arse, *che*,' said Alejandro. With his moustache and oily black hair, he could have been a tango singer.

With or without them, family life appeared to be proceeding somewhat chaotically. Alejandro's two young sons had occupied a row of seats and were using them like a trampoline. They were fat and screeched like piglets. The wives of Alejandro and Leandro had occupied a second row of seats and were deeply involved in reading the list of duty-free goods in the airline magazine.

Alejandro offered me a glass of champagne. 'Allow me to ask you one question,' he said. 'What are you doing going to Rio? You look the kind of person who should go to Paris, but the books you're reading are all about Brazil.' I told him that the newspaper I worked for had been on strike for three weeks so I thought it was time to take a holiday in the one place in Latin America I knew I wouldn't feel like working. Alejandro was drinking another glass of champagne. He found what I had to say so surprising that he spluttered half its contents over his dinner tray.

Leandro had blue eyes and a puffy face. He looked like a younger version of General Galtieri. He said, 'Hey, *che*, with an accent like that, you must be Spanish.'

'Half Spanish, half English,' I said. Alejandro laughed again. This time he was holding his glass so the laughter came out in a long cackle.

'Come on, *che*, give us another, you're Spanish. How can you be half and half of anything, let alone an *Inglés*,' Alejandro said.

I said that I was about as much Spanish as most Argentines and that a lot of Argentines were half 'Anglo'. Then Cecilia, Alejandro's three-year-old daughter burst out crying. She was sitting just across the gangway with her mother and Leandro's wife and small baby. While we were talking, Leandro had tried to forcefeed her some champagne.

'It tastes horrible, it tastes horrible,' Cecilia kept repeating between muffled sobs.

'A right pair of husbands you make,' said Leandro's wife.

'But it's good for you, my little nightingale,' said Leandro.

'Leave her alone, you drunk son of a bitch,' said Alejandro's wife, a leonine woman with bright red lipstick and sharp teeth. The two women picked up Cecilia and the baby and strutted off to the toilets.

Alejandro watched them go and then seemed completely to forget what he had been saying. 'Hey, *che*, let's get some duty free. There are bound to be a lot of French things,' he said.

They returned a few minutes later with cigars the size of pogo sticks in their mouths and a mountain of duty-free gifts under their arms. They sat down and began to play like little boys. 'Look at this, *che*,' said Leandro. He was flicking a gold lighter on and off. Alejandro was doodling on the airline magazine with a gold pen. They deposited the rest of the goods on my lap. Between them they had bought a

calculator, a bottle of Johnny Walker (Black Label), 400 Benson &
Hedges, four pairs of sunglasses, two boxes of Chanel No. 5, and an
assortment of Cuban cigars. 'Work it out, *che*, work it out. It's a real
bargain in dollars,' said Leandro. Alejandro then got to work on his
calculator . . .

Arriving at night in Rio was not like arriving in Paris at all. It was a
city you could smell on touchdown – a scent of sweet vegetation
mixed with roasted coffee. Most airports seem designed to make you
want to get out of them as quickly as possible. But Rio's was made
to hold you in a sensuous grip. It was not just the smell but also its
sounds. The flight information was given over the loudspeakers in a
soft coaxing voice that seemed to beckon you not so much to fly as
to bed. Buenos Aires was by contrast a city that had made a point of
anaesthetising any smells it might have once had.

Beyond the airport building, the sweetness was less of vegetation
than of diesel. It was hot and humid and very dark. There were black
figures everywhere. Kidge and I took a taxi – a VW Beetle owned by
Waldo Lima. He had a very thick neck and fat arms and seemed to
take up most of the vehicle. I only just managed to squeeze in behind
him. Taxis in Rio do not have door handles; they have ropes. So a
taxi-man has one hand on the steering wheel and another on the rope.
A taxi swerves from side to side because its driver is like the captain
of a sailing boat, tacking in response to the shifting directions of the
traffic. Waldo was driving thus when suddenly he braked. Ahead of
us, a set of coloured lights were blinking in the midst of a gathering
crowd. The crowd separated, letting through two men in white overalls
carrying a body on a stretcher. They were followed by an old woman
in a torn dress. She was walking with difficulty and was holding a
bloodied handkerchief to her face. Beyond there was a wrecked car
with a body dangling out of a door like a puppet.

'Fuck this, it's getting late,' said Waldo with a shrug of his shoulders.
Before the crowd had joined up again, he had taken advantage of the
space opened up by the ambulance and was once again driving like a
maniac through the dark night. It is not that I cannot remember more
of the journey. All my notes tell me is that I was so petrified by
Waldo's driving that I spent the bulk of the trip from the airport just
staring at his thick neck, flabby and grey like that of a hippopotamus.

I had the address of John Arden, a freelance Australian film-maker
I had befriended in Buenos Aires during the Falklands War. John had

performed the herculean task of ensuring that, for the three months the conflict lasted, all the best film material the Argentine military could produce on the islands found its way to the BBC, long before it was ever seen by the Argentines themselves.

John lived down a quiet street, well out of the city mayhem. 'You look worn out, mate,' he said as he stood in the doorway. Waldo was beside me holding my suitcase like a gangster. John and I had an argument with him about the cost of the taxi ride – Waldo wanted to charge me extra for the stop-over at the scene of the accident – and then he left.

That night I drank half a bottle of whisky as we watched *The Texas Chainsaw Massacre*. It was the video John had left us as a joke before he went to a party. It was about a man who ran amok in the United States in the 1960s, carving up his victims with a chainsaw. Each victim was stashed away in the basement of a house so that towards the end of the film bits and pieces of flesh were tumbling out all over the place like Jack in the boxes. I switched off after watching a scene in which someone was hung up on a cattle hook before having his legs sawn off. I finished the whisky and went straight to sleep. I had a dream about Waldo being a cannibal and wanting to chop me up for dinner.

The next morning we woke late, only to be greeted by John with the news that he had decided to have a party at home that evening. His guests were a small assortment of expatriates, mostly journalists who got drunk very quickly. One of them, who had a neutral English accent, described a party given by the Great Train Robber, Ronnie Biggs.

Ronnie was an introducer; he arranged his own publicity and allowed others to give it form and substance. He gathered together just about everyone who was anyone. Those who came to his parties were friends, contacts, hangers-on, anyone remotely desirous of having fun: government officials, writers, samba dancers, actresses, prostitutes, priests, petty thiefs, racketeers, diplomats (rumour had it that the British Ambassador was always invited and always politely declined) and, of course, journalists. Although everyone was carefully screened and sworn to secrecy, Ronnie was thought to be quite amenable to being interviewed as long as the price was right.

'It was a mixture of beggars' banquet and a tropical Dallas,' said the journalist. 'Everyone was remarkably well behaved, though.' I thought, if Ronnie was anything like his photographs, he was no doubt wearing a pair of floral bermudas and canvas shoes and looking – thanks to the nose job he had had done to avoid recognition by Interpol – like a movie star. But the journalist seemed too drunk to remember much detail.

Ronnie had come a long way since first helping his mates cosh an employee of British Rail to death and then heading off with two and a half million pounds in bank notes. The inhabitants of most of the countries he had run to had denounced him to intrepid journalists anxious for the 'scoop' of Biggs's arrest. But in Rio he had been saved by a steamy night of lovemaking with a local girl called Raimunda. The offspring of that brief encounter had been stamped with the characteristics of Ronnie's original nose; the rest of the baby was the mother's. But there was sufficient evidence of the union to ensure Brazilian nationality for Ronnie – as the 'naturalised' father of a child born in Brazil – and immunity for one of the most wanted of British criminals.

The British public, at least those who read the popular press, were outraged. But in Brazil, the Biggs story, with its photographs of the Anglo-Saxon Ronnie passionately embracing the half-caste Raimunda, was held up as an example of the country's 'enlightened' racial policy. By producing his baby, Ronnie, the Great Train Robber, had followed in the tradition of Luis Correa, a Portuguese sailor who, after being marooned in the fifteenth century near a remote Indian colony in north-east Brazil, populated an entire new village with his children and grandchildren. Modern Brazil, with its cauldron of different races including half-breeds and quarter-breeds of mixed Indian, white and negroid stock, is thought to spring from this prolific progenitor who went about impregnating the local population well before Portuguese rule had been formally established. Thus Ronnie – without a gene of colour in him – had contributed to that age-old sociological process by which the extramarital relations of white men with lower-class 'natives' had constantly added to the proportion of white blood in the Brazilian population as a whole. Raimunda was dusky, but baby Ronnie had turned out white enough to be a state senator.

We moved into the one block of apartments in a street filled with large houses. Most of the houses had high walls and security systems, but the apartment block had only a night watchman who was always sleeping whenever we came in late. From the roof of the block I could see the city in all its contrasts: in the distance, the ocean with its wisps of white foam, then the oily lakes a little further inland and a mass of buildings of different tone and shape, from wooden huts to tall skyscrapers made of glass. But somehow the constructions of the city seemed a mere appendix to the surrounding landscape thick with tropical vegetation.

One end of the street where we were staying smelt of fruit. It was there that one day I came across a young mulatto crushing the juice out of mangoes and guavas in a wooden casket. Near him was a large woman in a billowing skirt. I was watching her fingering a pile of bananas when down the road came a very thin tramp. He was about as black as the woman, but he was grinning from ear to ear and his eyes were bloodshot and protruded like a frog's. He was dancing a samba as he held an empty Coca-Cola tin to his right ear. I could not hear any music. But the woman laid the bananas to one side and started moving her hips; as she swayed from side to side, her skirt seemed to spread out across most of the shop front, covering it in a wave of coloured flowers.

The tramp shuffled over to where I was standing and began singing in a flat voice, 'Come and join me, come and join me, I'm the man from Coca-Cola Inc.' I said I couldn't hear the music. He put the can up to my right ear. I could hear the tapping of his fingers. I could smell the rum on his breath. And his face was just a mass of white teeth. The woman said, 'Don't take any notice of him, he's quite mad.' She pushed him to one side and then returned to fingering her bananas. 'Wilson has never killed anyone, or hurt anyone, or robbed anything. It's just that he likes smoking and drinking too much.'

'And women,' said Wilson, as he stumbled over to the woman, and buried his face in her huge breasts. I told Wilson his music was very good and then left him alone with his Coke can, cradled in the woman's lap like a child.

On another morning I got up very early and went down to the beach. It was dark when I left the apartment and when I reached the beach it was covered in mist. Treading on the sand, I imagined, was like walking on the moon. I had no idea of where I was or where I was going or if the beach really existed. So I sat down, listening to the waves lapping on to the shore, and waited for the mist to lift.

The mist lingered like a London fog. Then it parted just a little. I could hear a dog barking far away, and then a man's voice shout, 'Dio, Dio, come over here.' Somewhere a woman giggled, and then somebody was thumping the sand. From nowhere, two figures were running at me: as they came through the mist, they seemed to be floating as they ran. It was frightening to see them, growing bigger, blacker, in silence. I was about to get up and scream, when the figures stopped. Now their hands were moving in an arc, drawing rainbows in the morning dew, and thumping, thumping the sand. From behind me, I heard the sound repeated, almost on top of me and a jogger passed by me quickly. He had a Walkman wrapped around his ears. As the mist lifted, I saw hundreds of naked legs pacing, kicking, stamping, jumping, in a mass gymnastic display. This was midweek and along the seafront cars and buses were already making their way to the city's business centre, but the focus of activity was here on the beach. There was not a spotty shoulder or flabby stomach to be seen. It was all broad backs and hard biceps. It was hard to believe there was another side to Rio.

Favelas looked pretty, warm, and beckoning, but then I had always seen them from a distance. At night from a plane, I had gazed down on them. They looked like candles flickering on water. In daytime out of the apartment building, the *favela* was rusty coloured. Then at night-time again the *favela*, on the ridge across the valley, was filled with the soft light of lanterns. There was also a distant dog bark and the sporadic cry of a child.

We caught a taxi along the seafront and then walked to Vidigal, the largest *favela* of them all. This particular shanty town was set on a hill just behind the Sheraton Hotel. We were met by Father Jesus, a Spanish Jesuit. He was reading his breviary by a rubbish tip. He took us to a building where there was a school and a chapel and invited us to join him for Mass. The chapel was built like a garage – its walls decorated with children's drawings and slogans evoking the Church's social conscience. There were no chairs, so people either stood or sat around the altar – a bare table on which were set a jug, a wooden cross and some loaves of bread. There was a lot of singing, and when it came to 'Our Father' everyone stood in a circle and held hands.

'There is a greater sense of community here than in any neighbour-hood in Rio,' said Father Jesus. But he knew that in other *favelas* there was not so much a sense of community as of ghetto. Outsiders were quickly identified and disposed of. To be allowed in, you had to prove yourself a mugger or murderer. Thus, Ronnie Biggs was among the few non-Brazilian whitemen to have access to the rougher *favelas*. He had earned the respect of the inhabitants by pulling off one of the greatest train robberies in history and getting away with it. 'Heroes' like Biggs were created by the armed gangs – the *marginais* or marginal ones as they are euphemistically called by the Brazilians – who fought over the protection and domination of the *favelas*. Often these gangs would fight it out for days without anyone intervening. The police were usually part of the racket and the Church had beaten a tactical retreat to Vidigal. Whoever came out victorious ventured forth again into the outside world, robbing more banks and ensuring themselves of a still larger cut on drug sales and prostitution.

Occasionally the outside world played into their hands. I knew of a journalist, then the Rio correspondent of an English newspaper, who on arriving in Brazil at the start of his posting had rented himself a house which bordered the outer perimeter of one of Rio's most notorious *favelas*. The journalist, a veteran of rougher Third World places, calculated that the risk was worth the space and the view the house offered at what was then widely considered a bargain price. So enthused was he with the place that he moved in the Persian carpets he had picked up on his last posting and started drawing up plans to convert half the house into an art gallery. His plans were cut short brutally one night when a gang of *marginais* broke into the house with machine-guns, tied the journalist naked to his bed, and ran off with his money, his paintings and his Persian carpets.

In Vidigal, by the grace of God, things were different. The local community, helped by Father Jesus, had organised their own electricity and internal water supply, their own schooling and health service. The money that was used here came from the Church and the government. The funds might not have been so forthcoming had it not been for the recent visit of Pope John Paul II, who had been shown Vidigal by the authorities as the 'City of the Poor'. The military blamed the poverty on the unscrupulous behaviour of the foreign banks, conveniently forgetting that it takes two to create a debt.

We walked down endless alleyways and stopped off at numerous huts made of metal sheeting and rough wood. There were canaries in cages, and parrots on clothes lines, chickens pecking on bits of corn and children kicking footballs; there seemed to be few men around the place, but there were a lot of women sweeping their floors fastidiously. At the top of the hill was a small chapel, marking the place where the Pope had celebrated Mass. Inside was a small glass box containing a large gold ring with the inscription, 'This ring was donated by Pope John Paul II on the occasion of his visit to Vidigal.'

'Why didn't you sell the ring and use the money on the *favela*,'

I asked Father Jesus when we got back to the chapel. He told me that he had held a ballot on the subject of the ring and everyone in the *favela* had voted to keep it or give it to the city's museum. 'You see, it's not money people have here, it's social coexistence,' he said.

As we walked away from Vidigal I thought that here in a sense humanity had not so much progressed as turned full circle to the days when Brazil's underclass of Indians were herded together in their moneyless communities under the benign yet paternalistic rule of the Jesuit missions. These missions were in the end broken up by the *bandeirantes* and the Indians were taken off to forced labour, to places where the demand for more workers was more important than the kind of living quarters that could be created in the Brazilian wilderness. Father Jesus waved goodbye. He looked at peace with himself and others. But I was worried by the few men I had seen in Vidigal.

Perhaps some of the men were lurking in the shadows of the square just behind Copacabana beach. At night groups of them gathered and plotted. This was the area of Rio most tourists had read about in their guidebooks. When we were there it had been declared a virtual no-go area by the police. The police usually stood in pairs on either side of the square but nearly always walked round the perimeter. They told tourists they could cross it at their peril. We crossed the square. There was a smell of marihuana. Under the dim yellow light of a street lamp, a black figure was playing with a knife. He was standing near a night club advertising a live sex show. 'Fuckie, fuckie, good girls,' a voice hissed from the doorway. We were half-way across the square. I turned round and looked for the man with the knife. He was still there, white on black and covered in yellow haze. But we decided to run anyway and kept on running until we'd found the busiest terrace café on the seafront. Over a couple of *caipirinhas*, the local 'tonic' of lime juice and alcohol, we watched the street theatre of prostitutes haggling with the tourists. The prostitutes were tall, and wide-hipped. They were mostly mulattas who swaggered rather than walked. They operated in pairs and occasionally gathered in larger groups. They talked a lot, excitedly among themselves, as they touched up their make-up and rearranged their miniskirts.

At one point, one of these groups caught sight of a man of some distinction. He was wearing a navy blue jacket and a pair of beige slacks. He had been walking fairly briskly until he reached the group. Then he started walking more slowly. He kept looking at the ground, anxiously waiting for a shadow to follow him. I recognised Leandro Morandini, one of my companions on the Air France Jumbo. Two prostitutes caught up with him, one on either side, and took him by the arm. He nodded his head. The prostitutes nodded theirs. Leandro disengaged himself from their grip and started walking quickly. They caught up with him again, and this time one of them blocked his path while the other stood behind. For a moment Leandro was buried out of sight. When he re-emerged, his shirt was hanging out of his trousers and he was without shoes. Leandro looked distinctly harassed. The three began arguing again and then one of the prostitutes unstrapped a hangbag from her shoulder, stepped back and swung it in Leandro's face. It hit him hard across the nose. Then the other prostitute started running away. She was clutching a wallet in her hands. Her colleague went on swiping the man repeatedly with her bag. Locked in battle, they grappled and groped their way along the seafront. They passed packed terraces of people drinking *caipirinhas*, a man selling ice-cream, and a police box with no policeman. Then I watched them disappear into the night. They were followed by a posse of women in short skirts and high heels.

Within a few hours we were catching a slow tram up a steep mountainside to one of the highest peaks overlooking Rio. The tram left the beach behind and climbed between the *favelas*. At first it was filled with tourists. They sat intermingled with the washerwomen from the *favelas* who were carrying baskets of clothes. Then the washerwomen left and the tourists started taking pictures. When we reached the top of the mountain we lost them. The Corcovado, which the guidebook translated as a 'hunch-backed peak', was covered in thick fog and we searched blindly for the forty-metre-high statue of Christ the Redeemer whose huge arms stretch out to embrace the city of sin and compassion. We heard the tram move away and the high-pitched sound of Americans complaining they had not seen anything. We decided to sit and wait.

It was eerie, the silence and the fog and the fear of being discovered. Now that the tourists had gone I imagined a group of *marginais* gathering to mug me. I had been told that muggings near the Christ were as frequent these days as in Copacabana. Then the mist began to lift and we realised that the patch of ground we were sitting on was just a few feet away from the base of the statue. The tall robed figure – almost Virgin-like – revealed itself like a vision, which is probably what the person who carved it in the first place intended. The prostitutes disappeared into the night, the *marginais* hid in the *favelas*, the military ruled at a distance, but Christ the Redeemer was ever-present, lurking behind the clouds, and appearing when you least expected him.

John had said that if we ever had a free weekend we should go to Parati, a small colonial fishing town a few hundred kilometres south-west of Rio. He would take time off from his journalistic commitments and show us what he claimed was the 'most beautiful beach' in Brazil. I had come to Rio to escape from my journalistic commitments, but on our sixth day there we were joined in the apartment by two colleagues from my newspaper. One of them was Patrick, the son of Claud Cockburn, who was on his way to Moscow. We went for supper to a Japanese restaurant where we sat on the floor eating raw fish served out by mulattas posing as 'geishas', and argued about politics. We declared ourselves social democrats, labourites, environmentalists, anything but Thatcherites. We agreed that she seemed very remote to our South American experience. Beyond the Falklands, she seemed not to care a damn for it. We also laid bets on how long the strike at our newspaper would last and all hoped that it would be as long as possible so we could enjoy a lengthy holiday. I then rang up John and said that we were ready for Parati.

We set out in convoy, Kidge and myself in one car, John and his Brazilian girlfriend Flávia in another, and Oliver and Rosie, a local English couple, bringing up the rear. On the outskirts of Rio we stopped off by a hut overlooking the ocean and had a breakfast of fried fish and firewater. The beach there was already crowded with people playing ball games and exercising their limbs. Occasionally, hang gliders swooped down from a near-by cliff, narrowly missing our heads before plunging into the sea. There was a heavy scent of coconut oil.

'Just look at those women, doesn't it make you feel sick?' said Rosie. The women she had seen could not have been more than thirty between them. Each was wearing a small triangle between the thighs and a string over the crevice at the back. Two bits of material the size of buttons covered the nipples. Naked, they would have had very little else to show except the colour of their pubic hair. They were gyrating as they walked, as if in a slow-motion samba. Rosie stared out towards the ocean, but her gaze seemed to take in the whole of Brazil. 'Brazil's all right for men. They can fantasise their hearts out, kid themselves that these women are really asking for it all the time. But what is there in it for a woman when her arse can only waddle like a marshmallow?'

'The trouble is that most Brazilian men are gay,' Flávia said.

What was certainly true was that there had to be few places in the world where 'body culture', as Rosie preferred to call it, played such a central and exaggerated role as here. Gilberto Freyre, one of Brazil's best-known sociologists, had written volumes about the physical characteristics of the Indians, blacks and Portuguese in defence of what he considered the country's unique hybrid society. 'The milieu in which Brazilian life began,' wrote Freyre with all seriousness in his classic treatise *The Masters and the Slaves*, 'was one of sexual intoxication. No sooner had the European leaped ashore than he . . . became contaminated with licentiousness. The women were the first to rub themselves against the legs of these beings whom they supposed to be gods. They would give themselves to the European for a comb or a broken mirror.'

Freyre's writings have been strongly criticised as a racist simplification of a complex social, political and cultural history. But the definition of what constitutes Brazil in purely sexual terms or imagery has persisted in the country's mass culture: the heroines of Brazil's best-known twentieth-century novelist, Jorge Amado, spend more time making love than talking. In the United States Amado has earned a reputation less as a master storyteller than as a skilful, if exotic, weaver of sexy tales. Brazil's best-known film actress, Sónia Braga – she played the leading role in two of Amado's most popular screen plays, *Dona Flor e seus dois maridos* and *Gabriela* – is the quintessential mulatta Freyre saw 'invented' in the early days of colonisation. A woman of few words but sufficiently interesting sexually to the reader of *Playboy* magazine to be the ultimate fantasy of how a half-caste should perform. She was sexy in a crude 'jungly' kind of way, not at all like the usual Playmate of the Month. The contrast seemed to invoke the old Brazilian saying, 'White woman for marriage, negro woman for work, mulatto woman for fucking.' It was mulatto women that the Brazilian Tourist Board had on their posters suggestively licking on a straw, mulatto women tourists came looking for in their search for a primitive whore at carnival time.

'I don't know about the men,' said Flávia as we walked back to the cars, 'but I do know what a lot of us women feel. We don't like foreigners taking a fancy to us just because of our bodies. The Argentines are the worst – they cross the border convinced every Brazilian woman wants to jump into bed with them.'

John said the road to Parati was beautiful but long, the kind we might want to linger over. He and the others were anxious to get there as soon as possible. So we decided to split up the convoy and meet later. The road ran parallel to the ocean. It was lined with rubber trees, thick with foliage which was deep green and glistening in the sun after the rains. Below, the sand was very white and the water pale blue except where the rocks had made it darker or where the vegetation, left to itself, had grown beyond the land. There was a breeze blowing in from the ocean. We were thinking how clean and empty it all seemed after Rio when we suddenly saw a huge spider walking slowly across the road. I stopped the car and we watched its progress from a safe distance. It was covered in a thin coat of rough brown hair and had a hammer head and bulbous eyes. It was bigger than a man's foot and was dragging itself along a calculated if seemingly anarchic route, like a giant crab. Kidge, who had studied biology at school, guessed it was a tarantula and we walked rapidly back to the car.

We left the vegetation behind us, driving over a hill of coarse grass filled with wild flowers, and past an oil refinery built where there had once been a quiet fishing village with extraordinary views of the ocean. There was a big flame and clouds of yellowish smoke and the air was acrid. As we pondered on how the Brazilians had done far greater ecological massacres in the Amazon for the sake of economic progress, I was stopped by the police for driving without a licence.

Comissário Alves was a great hulk of a policeman. When one of his men brought me to see him, he was sitting behind a desk smoking a large, roughly rolled cigar. There was a wooden fan spinning from the roof. Lying in my teeth, I explained in Portuguese that I had left my driving licence on the beach and that it had since been stolen. Comissário Alves sucked deeply on his cigar and then gave me one of those black smiles that seem to cover a whole face. He said, 'Very well, then why didn't you report the robbery to the *delegacia policial*?'

'I was just about to,' I said.

'But you were driving past when we stopped you.' Comissário Alves had risen now. Standing he seemed to take up most of the room. He handed me a piece of paper on which was written the equivalent of 150 US dollars in two sets of 35,000 cruzeiros.

I asked him why he was fining me twice.

'This is why,' said Alves. He had picked up a dusty book and was shaking it as if it were a bible and he an evangelist. 'This is why: driving without a licence; driving a car without a licence.'

I asked – for Alves showed no intention of letting go of the book – whether the rules specified the fine for each offence. Alves looked at me, blew on his cigar and gave a big smile again. 'Aha, my friend, we are no longer talking about rules but about the meaning of charity. For you have no doubt heard that Brazil is the land of co-existence and compassion. So, you would like me to pardon you. Is that it?'

'Oh no I'm not asking for a pardon . . . no, perhaps I am,' I said.

'At last we understand each other,' Alves said, reaching out and embracing me. 'You pay one fine only and I'll tear up the piece of paper. Then we can forget this ever happened.'

When he had torn up the fine and thrown it in a waste bin, I handed him 20,000 cruzeiros. It was the final price we had haggled about over a cup of coffee.

'You look unhappy, my friend. You shouldn't. After all you come from a rich country. We are only poor here. We have to make our living somehow. But what's twenty thousand here or there? It's a memorandum of understanding, nothing more, the kind of stuff we sign with the International Monetary Fund . . . only promise you won't be a journalist and go writing about this afterwards.'

Parati, with its black-painted wooden shutters and whitewashed walls and coloured fishing boats, seemed little changed since the Portuguese had built it over three hundred years ago. It had that timeless, effortless air shared by any town in which the local authorities have had the good sense to ban traffic. We left the car by a large iron gate and walked through a rose garden to our hotel. Oliver and Rosie were sitting on a small veranda reading the newspapers. That evening, with John and Flávia, we all got very drunk as a result of a lengthy 'tasting' session in the local *cachaça* factory. We sat in a room smelling of wet wood and old tobacco drinking the firewater made from sugar cane. Outside in a courtyard a wild cat was chained to a cypress tree. When we stumbled out into the street, a horse-drawn cart was clattering on the cobblestones and an old tramp was sleeping by an oil lamp. Somewhere in the distance there was the sound of samba but it seemed far away. We zigzagged our way back towards the hotel.

John did not allow a hangover to disrupt our plans. The next day we climbed into his car and allowed him to take us to the ocean. 'No one has driven along this road before us. It's a secret path known only to hermits,' he said. We drove along a dirt track with deep pot-holes and ditches on either side. When the track climbed steeply we had to get out and push the car. When the track dipped downwards the car seemed to lose control. It slid on the loose stones and sand until the next upward gradient. It was like riding on a toboggan.

Once we had reached the ocean, John took us walking for miles along a deserted coastline. On the way, we met Wilson Santos. He had long black hair and an untamed beard and deep satanic eyes. He reminded me of a photograph of Charles Manson, the American hippie, after he had been arrested for the mass murder of some of the Hollywood jet set. Wilson was lying on a hammock and, quite literally, contemplating his navel. His son, Joãozinho, a small boy with bleached blond hair, was playing with a group of chickens. Beyond them both was the wife and mother, Aspásia. She had spiky hair, and was very thin. She was sitting on a wooden box, peeling some bananas.

Wilson and Aspásia were psychoanalysts by training. 'All that smoke and violence in São Paulo, no good, man, so get out, we just had to get out,' said Aspásia. For a dollar a head she had invited us to a lunch of banana cakes, 'seaweed soup', and coconut milk. I sat staring at her hairy legs, remembering a story I'd been told once about Norman Mailer. The author had gone to his doctor one day in New York to ask his advice about how to dry out. He had been drinking a lot and this had begun to affect his powers of concentration. Mailer picked on Brazil and flew to São Paulo, the only city other than Rio that tempted his curiosity. On the first night there, he got completely drunk. The next day he woke up. Bleary eyed, he looked out of the hotel window and saw for the first time the polluted city with tall buildings. 'Christ, it's Chicago,' he screamed. He took the next plane back to New York.

I asked Aspásia if she had ever read anything by Norman Mailer. 'We have no need of books here,' she said.

About two miles on from where Wilson and his family lived we found the most beautiful beach in Brazil. John couldn't tell us how he'd found it in the first place. He just said, 'That's it, the most beautiful beach in Brazil.' Down from the mountains the river had flowed and formed a clear-water lagoon behind the rocks; on the other side of these rocks, but enclosed by a further group of boulders, the waters of the ocean were similarly tamed. From the edge of the mountains, the vegetation leaned over the water of the first lagoon, and was reflected in pockets of dark shadow. There was a scarcely contained tension in the water with the river water pressing on the rocks and the waves of the sea occasionally gushing through the gaps. All around the white sand shimmered in sunlight.

From Parati, we drove back to Rio and caught a plane to Salvador, the capital of Bahia, the fifth largest city of Brazil, 1,700 kilometres further north. 'You can't understand Brazil, without going to Bahia,' Aspásia had said. She had also recommended that we should accompany her to São Paulo. But I had been there during a brief work tour in 1981 and felt there was nothing new for me to discover. It was a city that I had identified with work: *paulistas* said that the people of Rio, the *cariocas*, were superficial and flippant and beach bums; the *cariocas* said that São Paulo stank of pollution and bankers making money and children dying of malnutrition. I found that *paulistas* took themselves much too seriously. Salvador was a town I had read about. I was anxious to discover if the reality matched up. 'Salvador's population is about 1,050,000. It was founded in 1549, and was till 1763 the capital of Brazil. Most of the 135 churches, the fortifications, and some other buildings date from the 17th and 18th centuries.' That much I had read about in my guidebook. The Salvador I wanted to put to the test was the Salvador in which Dona Flor had been haunted by the erotic spirits of her late first husband, Vaidinho, and 'where these and other acts of magic occur without startling anybody'.

Dona Flor's creator, Jorge Amado, had described Salvador as a town where 'sex ran rife'. Gilberto Freyre, the sociologist, had written about the 'infectious cheerfulness of the Bahians . . . their grace, their spontaneity, their courtesy, their heart and contagious laughter. In Bahia one has the impression that every day is a feast day.'

We followed Dona Flor's footsteps out of the church of São Francisco and into the square of Terreiro de Jesus. The urchins, the offspring of the whores of that district, were there much as Amado had described them. They were 'scattered about the overflowing square, running between the legs of itinerant photographers, trying to swipe an orange, a lime, a tangerine, a hot plum, a *sapoti* from the vendors' baskets'. They were beating out the syncopated rhythms of the samba on empty guava paste tins, making lewd remarks about Kidge's 'fine bum'. (The Brazilian word for a woman's bottom is *bunda*. The word evokes something wholesome, and to many Brazilians, it is more important than any other part of the anatomy.)

There was a man holding a bucket with a snake round his neck. He was a street magician trying to get two urchins to help him make huge pieces of 'magic bread' disappear. The bread was shrivelled and mouldy, but the magician was applauded by a small crowd every time he stuffed the stale flour down the boys' throats. In the bread went, roll after roll, like handkerchiefs into a hat. For about two minutes the boys swallowed every piece whole without uttering a sound. Then suddenly one of them began to choke. He coughed and spluttered and his eyes opened up like huge planets, and all the time the magician with his snake around his neck tried to force more bread down. The snake perked its head up and squirted a jet of green liquid all over his master's arm, and, in that very instant, the boy was sick into the bucket. Everyone applauded.

In another corner of the square, by a convent, there was a group of half-naked blacks, frantically beating some drums with their hands. Their bodies were covered in sweat and their eyes reflected the frenzy of their beating, which was getting louder and louder as if working up to an explosive climax. In front of them another, larger crowd had gathered. They were all blacks except for a few young tourists. One blond and tall German seemed unable to maintain his balance in the surging crowd of dancing people. As he was pushed forward, a black woman leaned back and began rubbing herself against him. He tried to put his arms around her but as he did so he was suddenly jolted violently from the side. It was all a distraction which allowed a third protagonist to slice the money belt around the boy's waist before merging back into the crowd. On the steps of the convent, a Swedish girl in short pants and sandals was dancing with two black youths. One of them was licking her back like an ice-cream; another was whispering in her ear.

Suddenly, Salvador struck me as rather nasty, like Brixton or Notting Hill at carnival time. The Salvador Amado and Freyre had written about was a tropical jungle of scented flowers and blazing colours; Amado's characters were humorous, sensuous beings, their love play echoing a world that was both warm and exuberant. But the Salvador I now experienced seemed little more than the consequence of three hundred years of inequality and racial abuse. Freyre has written about the explosions of racial hatred and cultural earthquakes that have periodically shattered Brazil's veneer of co-existence and compassion: cultural earthquakes 'on the part of oppressed cultures bursting forth in order not to die of suffocation and breaking through the encrustations of the dominant culture that they might be able to breathe'. Such was the case with the negro movement of Bahia in 1835 in which the sons and grandsons of former slaves erupted into an orgy of messianic violence. There hadn't been anything on such a scale since. But it was no coincidence that Salvador now had one of the highest crime rates in Brazil. Salvador's carnival, unlike Rio's, belonged to its people and was regarded as much too dangerous for outsiders. The only visible reminder of the last carnival when I arrived in Salvador was a boldly painted graffiti across the walls of the convent where the Swedish girl reclined. 'Black Power', it proclaimed.

There were many tourists in Salvador when we were there. They were mostly Argentines. Few of them tempted fate by crossing Terreiro de Jesus. Instead they sat in one of the numerous tower-block hotels along the road to the airport, or else in the Convento do Carmo, a former Carmelite convent which had been converted into a luxury hotel in the old quarter of town. In 1620, Portuguese and Spanish troops were billeted in the Convento do Carmo before battling with the Dutch in a war between Empires. Now the cells had been converted into bedrooms with TV, and the cloisters into a swimming pool and adjoining restaurant. We looked for the voluptuous mulattas whom Vaidinho, Dona Flor's rakish husband, had spent the last hours of his life bedding and gambling with; we investigated the private alleyways that I had heard led to the spellworkers and voodoo centres of *macumba*, the smell of chicken's blood and incense, and the altar of Oxóssi, one of the pagan gods worshipped by the Africans. But that year, the whores of Salvador's red-light district were withered pathetic creatures – old women with running make-up and torn skirts, and their daughters – mostly drug addicts, the precursors of Brazil's Aids epidemic. The only mulattas we saw were in a folklore show the local tourist board put up on alternate nights in a restaurant close to the convent. They danced a samba while their men did a 'war dance'. The evening included a buffet of fifty Bahian dishes – a 'sample of the typical food eaten by Bahians', announced the menu. We sat in a restaurant – self-billed as the most important centre of Afro-Brazilian cooking in Brazil – chewing and burping our way through dishes I had seen no whore or urchin eating. One of the finest offerings was the *acarajé*. 'It is made of beans (*feijão-fradinho*) grated on the stone, with a dressing of onions and salt. It is heated in a clay frying pan into which is poured a little *dendê* oil.' There was a dish cooked in palm oil and manioc, a chicken tossed in peanut butter, turtle soup, rice pudding, tapioca, fried bananas . . . the banquet seemed endless. Dona Flor had taken to such cooking to get her mind off Vaidinho once her late husband began to haunt her. I felt Bahia was being packaged. So when the porter at the hotel came up one evening and asked me if I'd like to go and see some *macumba*, I told him we were booking out next morning.

I have no doubt that as we stuffed ourselves at the banquet, all the *orixás* or high priestesses of the occult had assembled to bury the spirit of Vaidinho that lurks in each one of us. 'Lightning and thunder, whirlwind, steel against steel, and black blood . . .' Oxumaré in the form of a huge snake, the goddess of the Sea, Iemanjá dressed all in blue, with her long hair of foam and crabs, and all the deities of Angola and the Congo. I was sure that devils and all those born on the wrong side of the bed covers were at that moment floating out to sea, just as Amado had written, along with their houses and mansions and that in the Terreiro de Jesus 'fish were sprouting among the flowers and stars were ripening in the trees'. But as surely as it all existed, it was also out of sight, behind the scenes, held in reserve. It was pouring with rain as we left the folk show. A man in a raincoat with a loud Texas drawl went up to one of the mulattas and said, 'Why, babe, you sure are beautiful.'

We caught a ferry to Itaparica, a small tropical island off the coast of Bahia. The guidebook said that Itaparica was the first stretch of land spotted by the Portuguese when they set out to discover Brazil. In Spain I had spent much of my life near Palos from where Columbus set off on his voyage to America, so I wanted to end this voyage here in Itaparica where the old world had linked up with the new. Like Luis Correa – the washed-up sailor and primogenitor of the Brazilian race – I settled with Kidge into a tree hut surrounded by palm trees and ocean. Our only neighbours were three parrots and a monkey who spent most of the day trying to imitate each other. Across the bay, we watched three fishermen punting silently from long dug-out canoes. There was also a group of young boys wading through the shallow water with giant octopuses dangling from the tips of primitive harpoons. The boys had long hair and were naked. They looked like hunters returning from a hard-fought battle. Then I got a message from London that the strike at my newspaper was over and we flew back to Buenos Aires.

—5—

DOWN THE MINE

A woman I knew in Buenos Aires told me this story about her lover.

Miguel was waiting for the *colectivo* in his uniform. He saw the number 29 turn the corner at the end of the street. It was the one he knew best because it was driven by his friend Raúl. He never took another one on the way home. It was a dark night and very rainy and the number 29 looked like a dragon wading through the river. It was coming very fast as if Raúl hadn't seen him standing there in the shelter, so Miguel stepped out on to the street, his feet falling into a pool of water as he did so. Then he saw that it was not Raúl looking at him from the face of the dragon, but four kids. They had long hair and were screaming 'Hijo de puta' and were holding machine guns out of the door. Miguel went for his pistol when the shooting had already begun. The first bullet made a big hole just above his heart. He swung once, twice, three times. They shot him in the back, twice in the lungs, and the force was so great that it pushed him three metres across the street. He lay there, still as an angel, with four big holes cut into his uniform. They looked like the burns of a cigar butt. His sister was the first in the family to hear about it. In the neighbourhood there was suddenly a lot of talk about a policeman being shot and she said, 'Oh, please God, I hope Miguel is safe. He should be home by now.' But it was Miguel. We found him lying in a river of blood and he died at dawn before I could say goodbye. He was my *compañero*, never said a bad word, never hurt anyone, podgy and dark he was, a real *gordo* negro. That year so many people died. They took them out of bed, interrupted their meals, picked them off the *colectivos*, shot them in the street. They fell like flies. Aurora, who had watched it happen, said they had opened his hand and taken his pistol. They didn't want his watch or his wallet, just his pistol.

That December in Buenos Aires, it was so hot that a man, dressed as Father Christmas, stripped down to his t-shirt. He was walking down

Florida Street smoking a cigarette and handing out plastic soldiers. He had told me he was collecting for a children's charity, but I followed him to a bar near the Richmond and watched him use the money on some coffee and cakes. At the airport the next day, there was an American tourist – silver haired and dressed impeccably in pale grey slacks – who put a fifty dollar bill in his ticket before passing it across the counter. 'I haven't got a reservation, but I need to go on this plane,' he said. It was all money and crowded planes that December in Buenos Aires. With triple-figure inflation and the local currency heavily devalued on the local black market exchange, the only place left in the world where inflation was higher and the currency weaker was Bolivia. But when people said they were going to Bolivia, they meant La Paz. So we bought tickets instead for a town north-east of the capital called Santa Cruz. It seemed far away on the map. And anyway Che Guevara, possibly the most romantic revolutionary of the twentieth century in spite of being an Argentine, had been there.

In the lowlands of the province of Santa Cruz it was the rainy season. The air was as the asthmatic Che had suffered it, humid and filled with the sweet smells of tropical vegetation. As we drove into the town from the airport, there were some shanty huts sprawled out near the highway. 'People from Vallegrande, where El Che died,' said the taxi-man, looking at the huts sadly.

Vallegrande was a day's trip away by bus, but in the fifteen years since El Che had died, more than forty per cent of the population of Vallegrande – about 3,000 people – had moved to the outskirts of Santa Cruz, pushed away by their own poverty and pulled by the illusion of oil wealth. The dream had proved shortlived. The local barons had moved into the cocaine trade and the oil had 'dried up'. 'Much money there is here but the pueblo doesn't see it,' said the taxi-man. From then until the moment I left Bolivia, I had the overriding impression of a country facing terminal decay. And I understood, coming as I did from Buenos Aires, why it was that Che had met his fate here.

Santa Cruz was a boom town that had fizzled out. The hotel we stayed at had an overgrown garden and a swimming pool with broken tiles and green water filled with active insects. It was run by an English expatriate and his servile Bolivian wife. The Englishman had bulbous eyes and his complexion was dyed with an alcoholic ruddiness. He spent most of the time in the shade of a rotting palm tree, drinking

Cinzano. His wife followed the hotel clients wherever they went with a matronly sense of perfection. While her husband slept she would do the sweeping and change the sheets; when he drank, she'd go into the kitchen and start cooking. Neither of them said very much. They both seemed cut off from the world, although their reasons for being so were different: she, because of her shyness and years of submissiveness; he, because of an underlying misanthropy, the roots of which I only partly discovered.

Only once did he talk to me and that was when I asked him how we could get out of Santa Cruz. He told me he had left England twenty-six years before and had come to Bolivia to sell helicopters, exactly to whom he wouldn't say. He did however talk about the cocaine barons. 'They're more respected round here than the Archbishop, command more troops than the most senior General, are more powerful and influential than the President himself. And the cheek of it is that they all send their sons to English public school,' he said one afternoon as he sat dissecting a mango. 'There used to be a lot of money here, but this government is no good, you know . . . Ah, but you said you wanted to get out of Santa Cruz. I can tell you I arrived twenty-six years ago and I've been trying to get out ever since.' He laughed very loudly when he said this, and his laughter echoed around the hotel, but it was a laugh that had no joy in it. He then offered me a Cinzano and suggested I should hire a plane.

In the centre of Santa Cruz, red roofs sloped downwards over the sidewalks and were supported by wooden pillars, making it seem like a Wild West town. But beneath this veneer of eccentricity, Santa Cruz was quintessentially South American. Occasionally across the square would walk a member of the 200,000 odd community who had struck it rich fiddling with the exchange rates and monopolising the country's exports of coca, oil or tin. He would be dressed in a light blue suit and wearing very shiny black shoes and holding a cigar in one hand. He was always going somewhere, bathed in a look of supreme self-importance, nodding knowingly to the key characters in the town drama: the lawyer's clerk, the policeman, the bank manager and the priest. Bolivia was a country of six million people, but the tone and pace of towns like Santa Cruz were dictated by the man in the light blue suit, and the scrawny inhabitants who were propped up against the walls doing nothing at all except smoke stale tobacco were merely pawns.

Santa Cruz deteriorated the further away you walked from the town centre. Old men surrounded by empty bottles slept like crumpled sacks in doorways of half-ruined buildings. Long lines of people waited outside a shop selling nothing but chickens. Because of inflation, shopkeepers had taken to hoarding their goods, and the network of distribution had broken down. It was New Year's Eve but no one seemed to have the energy to celebrate it. Near the hotel, a bar also owned by the Englishman was offering a glass of champagne at eight dollars a head, but the town's elite stayed away and the square was empty.

On New Year's Day, it was pouring with rain and the only public building in Santa Cruz that offered shelter was the cinema. It was showing *Gremlins* by Stephen Spielberg. Billed as a 'children's movie', it told the tale of some dwarf reptiles who on making contact with water would reproduce frantically. When dry, a gremlin was soft and cuddly like that other Spielberg invention, ET. But when it was wet, the new-born Gremlin turned evil and homicidal. It seemed to be always raining in the American town just like in Santa Cruz. Little devils, moreover, formed part of Bolivian culture. So it was easy for the audience to identify with the violence of *Gremlins*. The women who yesterday had waited in the rain for chickens, now sat with their children eating peanuts. They clapped loudly whenever the human hero of the film exterminated a gremlin by putting him through the mincer or baking him in the microwave.

If a gremlin had appeared on the streets of Santa Cruz on New Year's Day, he might have been carved up and cooked for dinner although it is more likely he would have been proclaimed President. Bolivia had had eight Presidents in three years, so politics had become part of the country's fantasy. No one had bothered to take down the posters of an election that had taken place months ago. In the midst of economic collapse and rumours of an imminent coup, it was the face of Hernán Siles Suazo, an old man with the look of a pedantic university Professor, that stared down on the streets and proclaimed that he was the National Revolutionary Movement. 'WE ARE THE FUTURE', boasted the old man.

Near the square, there was a corner shop selling tourist posters of Che Guevara. 'In the countryside some of the peasants still think he's Christ and may return one day. But for me it's just good business. I'm getting ready for 1987, the twentieth anniversary of his death,' said Don Horacio, the shopkeeper. By the hotel, someone had scribbled 'BANZER RETURNS'. General Banzer had staged a military coup in

1971. Seven years later he had organised national elections so blatantly fraudulent that even the military was forced to declare them annulled. The graffiti reminded the population that the local airport had been built by General Banzer.

'Life was much better under Banzer,' said Lucía, a Bolivian teacher who was staying at the hotel. 'The only difference is that whereas before only a few Generals plundered the country, now democracy means everyone fighting for a piece of a stale cake. Look around you, all you've got is a dying country. Food queues and more food queues and bank notes useless as confetti.'

'What about Che?' I asked.

'He was a middle-class Argentine doing what middle-class Argentines like to do – give orders to other Latin Americans,' said Lucía.

And yet virtue had been made out of disaster, and a myth had been born which stirred imaginations all the way from the backstreets of Lima to the Paris barricades of 1968 and London's Kensington High Street, where a boutique selling mini-skirts had been named after him. Che's six-month campaign through the hills and jungle of Bolivia, from where he had hoped to set the continent aflame, had proved a revolution in reverse. The more Che and his band of Cubans and Bolivians advanced, the greater the ease with which the military imposed its will and picked them off one by one. Che's personal diary reads not so much as a testimony to revolutionary perseverance but as a chronicle of a death foretold for a band of incompetent boy scouts. Che was captured one Sunday afternoon in October 1967, after being wounded in one leg and suffering from a bad attack of asthma. Secretly an army Colonel supervised his execution. Had Che been cremated there and then, the myth might not have survived for so many years. But the military's own arrogance allowed for Che's rehabilitation. His body was taken to the near-by town of Vallegrande and laid out in the local laundry.

By displaying the dead Guevara in such ignoble circumstances, the military and the CIA had hoped to end once and for all the prospect of revolution in South America by killing not just the man but also the myth. And yet the plan backfired miserably. With his long hair swept back from his bearded face, and his eyes slightly open and glazed, El Che looked very beautiful in death, and photographers from all over the world who had converged on the small town recorded the figure of a contemporary Christ on the verge of resurrection. Within a year the face of Che was being held up high behind the Paris barricades, and by the early 1970s Guevarism had become the popular manual for guerrilla movements throughout South America. Subsequent dictators learnt their lesson. Their opponents were not placed on show in laundries, they simply 'disappeared'.

On the day that Lucía's cynicism began to rub off on me I decided finally to leave Santa Cruz. I too had put up a poster of El Che over my desk during my school days and toyed at university with the idea that violence could be noble. As a Catholic I had looked on Che as a theologian of liberation. In Buenos Aires there had been a day when Kidge and I had driven out across the prairie, to marvel at the country estate owned by the Guevara family, and which Che had voluntarily renounced. While I worked as a journalist, my commuter train would drop me off each morning by the platform Che had run along one day, dressed in fatigues and shouting, 'I am a soldier of America.' Now in Bolivia my hero's image was being punctured. 'Not even Christ was perfect,' I told Lucía before paying our hotel bill. The Englishman took my money, like a British Rail ticket collector, without expression or acknowledgement, as if he had never seen me.

On the way to the airport the taxi-man said, 'You've heard the news? There's been a plane crash near La Paz – an Eastern airliner flying from Asunción. It seems the yankees have been punished by Illimani.'

Mount Illimani is one of the highest peaks in the world, dominating the main approach to La Paz by air and featured in most tourist posters. But for many Bolivians, still steeped in the animism of the ancient Indian cultures, Illimani was a god who had the power of retribution over man's impudence. Illimani was more feared than any General, more deserving of popular respect than El Che, less easy to ignore than that other god the priests talked about. The *Yanquis* – as the Americans were called by Latin Americans who didn't like them – took photographs of Illimani for *National Geographic Magazine*, but they didn't believe in its spiritual powers. Why should they if it was they that had largely determined the fortunes of Bolivia through their management of the country's financial borrowing and their manipulation of the armed forces. But now the Eastern airliner had gone down and the people of Bolivia were privately celebrating. In a test of strength between gods, Illimani had won, killing the high priestess of American imperialism. There were fewer than thirty passengers on the plane, but one of them was the American Ambassador's wife. 'THE MAJESTIC ILLIMANI CLAIMS ITS LATEST VICTIM', proclaimed the headline of a local afternoon newspaper, thus confirming that the ritualistic sacrifice had indeed taken place.

I was relieved that we were booked on a Bolivian airline. Although it was rumoured to have one of the worst safety records in Latin America, I reckoned that God would be on our side now that the battle had been fought and won. The approach to La Paz was none the less one of the most nerve-racking experiences of my life, with the plane having to turn sharply to avoid being swallowed by the massive snow-covered mountain, before landing on the highest runway in the world.

Soroche is the name given to the altitude sickness that engulfs you on landing at La Paz's El Alto airport. It made us feel dazed and queasy until we were well embarked on our descent to the city. La Paz had been carved out of the mountain with a giant spade. The various layers of the city represented the social strata of its inhabitants like an opera house, so most of the Indians lived in the upper terraces, the mixed races and Indian traders in the middle circle, and the business and political class in the 'stalls' – the city centre with its high-rise blocks built on the base of the canyon.

We booked into a small hostel that was on the border of the Indian quarter and well away from the modern blocks. It was filled with students with knapsacks who had flown halfway across the world. On the noticeboard, a bankrupt English teacher was offering a volume of Dickens for $50; a Frenchman, a cheap ticket to Paris; and two Brazilian girls, companionship. The hostel was run by two brothers who looked like younger versions of Che Guevara. One of them seemed to spend most of the time on the telephone discussing politics, while the other used his calculator to work out impossible sums of conversion whenever one of his foreign clients came to pay a bill. 'I'm afraid the bank's run out of notes,' he announced one evening when Bolivia's inflation reached 1,300 per cent. That night a group of Indians sat in the foyer offering ponchos and flutes as barter.

'How can we get some money?' I asked the brother with the calculator. He told me I should go to Camacho Street, where I could exchange my dollars on the black market.

The next day was Epiphany, the Feast of the Three Kings, an appropriate anniversary to go looking for gifts. On the way to Camacho Street, once we had manoeuvred our way through the labyrinth of cobbled alleyways that characterise the quarter, we passed a long line of Indians waiting at a bus stop. Walking any distance in

La Paz makes you a little nauseous, so we stopped off at a small bar and ordered some coca tea. 'The state bus company announced yesterday that it is so bankrupt it no longer has any spare cash to run its vehicles. But the Indians don't read newspapers and no one's bothered to tell them. They've been waiting most of the morning,' said the waiter.

A few blocks along the road, on the edge of 'modern' La Paz, stood the old colonial church of San Francisco, where more crowds had formed. On the steps of the church stood hundreds of people clutching plaster-cast baby Jesuses. Their shapes and sizes, like those of the city's buildings, varied according to the status of their owners, so the white, well-dressed parishioners had large-sized Jesuses dressed in lace and pearls, while the Indians had thin little ones in rags. Such social demarcations were lost once the gigantic wooden doors of the church were opened by invisible hands, and the crowd stampeded through them. Soon hundreds of pilgrims were pushing and shoving each other as they scrambled towards the benches. At one point, a priest in a black cloak appeared at the high altar. He was bespectacled and twitched nervously. 'There is no need to rush. This year I intend to do a communal blessing so that no one will be left out,' he said, before leaving as suddenly as he had appeared. Later, once the congregation had settled into their seats, he returned, dressed in a silver-lined chasuble. In his vestments he looked more assured and when he stood in front of the altar, he began to lead the congregation through the rosary. Above him the ceiling of the church was decorated in ornamental gold, on which had been carved scenes of Indian mythology mixed with Christian symbols: there were fields of corn, reptiles and naked saints struggling together in a heavenly orgy. To his side was a bloody and broken Christ figure and a statue of the Virgin Mary, lily white and illuminated in striking contrast to the wasted, dark-skinned peasant women genuflecting before her. The women were holding out their hands in supplication while their menfolk withdrew up the aisle, heads bowed and hats held across their genitals. When the blessing of the Jesuses was over, the Mass began but, although it was a holiday of obligation, I thought it best to leave.

Camacho Street had no gold or incense, it was just four blocks of anonymous grey concrete buildings, a newspaper stand and a bank. All the offices and the bank seemed closed, but along the pavement there were groups of women leaning against the wall or sitting on stools. They wore hats and long dresses, some were reading news-papers, others were playing cards. They were old and unpainted and quite unassuming. Only one woman struck me as remotely sinister. She was very fat and wore a black pair of sunglasses, and from the moment we began walking down the street she followed us like a hawk. 'Hey, mister, you want to sell some American dollars?' she said when she had come up close. Her breath smelt vaguely of alcohol and she had a slight limp which became more pronounced the faster we walked. When we had reached the end of the street, the road widened into an avenue and I could see that, except for Camacho Street and the Church of San Francisco, La Paz *moderno* was very empty. I was tempted just to walk on because I knew that Camacho Street was like a prison beyond whose boundaries the women would never venture. We had stopped, the woman, Kidge and I, at the corner. She stood there panting. 'No pesos in the bank, mister, *Señora* has plenty, buy buy . . . I give you best price in town.' I gave her a hundred dollars in bills of twenty. She began to walk away. For some reason I trusted her when she said she was just going to the newspaper stand. She returned carrying a large canvas bag.

'Mister, your *cambio*,' she said. From the bag she began to produce large wadges, about six inches thick, of peso notes. The first six packs I distributed between my pockets; the next six I gave to Kidge, who put most of them in her handbag. But the packs kept coming out of the woman's bag like one of those magician's tricks with handker-chiefs. 'This is absurd, I can't go round town like this,' I said. By now I was holding another twenty packs in my arms, and Kidge had started to lay hers on the pavement. 'You'll have to give us a larger denomination . . . fewer notes,' insisted Kidge. 'No problem, mister, we finish now. *Rápido* because I think police come,' said the woman before she handed me the bag and limped quickly away.

We were arrested by two khaki-clothed policemen with shaved heads. They collected the notes that were on the pavement like street sweepers, before asking us quite politely to accompany them. I looked down Camacho Street. It was empty. With no witnesses and both policemen fingering their pistols, we clearly had little option other than to accompany them to wherever they wished to go.

The nearest police station was an old Spanish palace with crumbling plaster and rusty grilles and a staircase lined with banisters of dark wood, at the top of which was the Chief Commissioner's room. The Commissioner was overweight, moustachioed and wearing braces. He was sitting, slightly elevated on a velvet chair, reading a newspaper. The room was bare except for two hangings which took up most of the wall space: a painting of a General in gala uniform, and a poster with the motto: 'THE POLICE ARE THE HONOUR OF THE NATION.'

Comisario Vázquez welcomed us to Bolivia and wished us a happy Epiphany before asking what he could do for us. 'It is not the *Ingleses* who have come, but we who have brought them,' said one of the skinheads.

'Aha, so you are under arrest? What for – drugs?' Vázquez asked sharply. His subordinates explained the cause of arrest. Vázquez smiled and then said, 'I see your problem, mister, there is no money in the bank today. But you know the black market is strictly forbidden, Camacho Street is a no-good street with no-good women.'

Vázquez stood up and began to pace up and down, casting furtive glances at Kidge with scarcely concealed lust. Eventually he came over to me and took my passport. He looked at each page carefully. 'So you are an *Inglés*, I thought you were an *Argentino*.'

Finally Vázquez told us we were free to leave. 'Only don't go back to Camacho or then I really will have you arrested.'

He walked with us on to the landing at the top of the stairs and, kissing Kidge's hand, added the postscript, 'Anyway, if you're ever with any problems of changing dollars come to me. I'll give you a better rate than the women of Camacho.' He then hitched his trousers up, grunted, and walked back into the building.

Moments later, once we had rounded the corner and the police station was out of sight, we looked into our respective bags. They were still stuffed with notes. Out of sheer nervous relief we both burst out laughing.

'What on earth are we going to do with all these notes?' said Kidge. 'Spend them, I suppose.'

So we went searching for more coca tea in the depths of a street market we had passed on the way down to San Francisco. We found an old shop filled with ponchos where teas were advertised and ordered three cups each. In our innocence we hoped that by so doing we would get the sense of elation and self-confidence we had got from the time we had snorted cocaine as students. But tea consisted of a single leaf floating in hot water and each cup was as tasteless as the next. We began eating the leaves. They were bitter and chewy but totally ineffectual. It was hard to imagine that these insipid bits of plant were the raw material for the most lucrative drug trade in the world. Only afterwards were we told that the Indians we had seen chewing on their coca before trudging up the hill, laden like beasts of burden, had first deposited a ball of lime in their mouths, without whose properties the coca leaf would never 'activate'.

'*La coca* is for those with different gods,' said the woman who brought me out of my ignorance the day before we left La Paz. She was shrouded in a shawl of coarse wool and her hair was grey and matted and fell over her shoulders. She ran a little stall in the Indian quarter. The woman was a *curandera* – an old witch doctor who believed in the healing properties of herbs and animals. At the door to her stall were some giant jamjars filled with foetuses of something half-way between a rabbit and a dog. She told me they were llamas taken from the wombs of their mothers while they were still alive and pickled in vinegar. An unborn llama was to a Bolivian what a horse-shoe is to a Welshman – a good luck charm which they hung over the entrance to their houses.

Our escape route from La Paz was plotted by Roxanne, a young travel agent whom a friend in Buenos Aires had recommended. 'Rox-anne will get you anywhere you want, even if it means walking on water,' he had said. Roxanne was trying to do three things at once and none of them very well when we first met her on a day when it poured with rain and parts of La Paz were flooded. She was having to deal with a smouldering electrical wire that had just short-circuited in the rain; she was picking up the phone and speaking to her dentist's secretary, cancelling a lunchtime appointment; she was tearing at her black Afro hair-cut and cursing the day she'd decided straight hair was out of fashion. 'You wanna travel,' she said in an American hispanic accent she'd picked up on a brief visit to New York. 'How about La Ruta del Che – sleeping and eating like Guevara did and following the route to La Higuera? No one has ever done it since he died, but then no Westerner thought he'd see Mao's tomb until he'd walked the long wall of China. How about it?'

I said that I still felt pretty romantic about Che.

'El Che is only taken seriously in Bolivia by the extremists. The left want him for a revolution and the military use the anniversary of his death to remind the people that it was the glorious armed forces that saved the fatherland from foreign mercenaries,' said Roxanne before excusing herself on the grounds that she was late for her psychoanalyst.

That evening Roxanne led us through the backstreets of the Indian quarter. They were filled with the echoes of distant voices, and smelt of coriander. We passed an old drunk kicking an empty crate, and at one point narrowly missed burial under a pile of vegetable peelings being emptied from an upstairs window. We saw a rat scuttle across the cobblestones before disappearing through a doorway, and a dog limping with his tail between his legs up a hill. Otherwise the town seemed to have closed down until the morning. We walked down a street so narrow that the old stone buildings seemed almost to touch each other, and descended into a poorly lit basement bar. The scene that confronted us instantly dispelled the mystique of our evening ramble. It was packed out with tourists wearing ponchos and woollen hats. 'I call this the United Nations,' Roxanne said. Looking around I saw what she meant. There were Italians and Frenchmen, Brazilians and Germans, and at a table near the stage two bearded Argentines eyeing two English girls dressed in brown overalls. No one really seemed to be taking much notice of the Bolivian women who had taken to the stage dressed in frilly skirts and coloured capes to do a 'traditional Indian dance' routine.

I asked Roxanne about the United Nations. She said, 'Oh, no doubt, you *Ingleses* are the coldest, the French are the most demanding, the Germans the most boring, and the Italians and Brazilians the most fun.'

'And the Argentines?'

'What about the Argentines?' she said, as she ordered the waiter to bring another bottle of wine.

'You left them out,' I said.

'Oh, the Argentines, just look at them, they're so arrogant, they think we owe them a favour. You know even I find it difficult to believe El Che came from Argentina.'

The Argentines had asked the English girls for a dance. On stage the women in frilly skirts and coloured capes had been replaced by a group of men playing an assortment of Andean flutes and drums in an ever-quickening beat. The faster the group played, the more excited the Argentines became, tossing the English girls into an improvised rock and roll. 'Who do you think you are, darling, John Travolta?' said Vanessa, a university student on her year off. She was well built and rather pretty and seemed to be the focus of attention for both the Argentines. But when one of them tried to touch her breasts, she stopped dancing and went back to her seat. The Argentines and the English girls were still arguing half an hour later when we decided to leave. By then the women in frilly skirts and coloured capes had returned. Their hair was now collected in long plaits and they waved a pair of silk handkerchiefs in front of them as they dragged their feet around the stage and issued a high-pitched wailing sound. It was as incomprehensible to me as Chinese opera, although their voices were soon overtaken by Roxanne's departing comment, 'Look, it's Malvinas round two.'

Vanessa had just thrown a glass of wine at John Travolta.

We left the hotel very early one morning before sunrise after leaving several wads of peso notes in payment for our stay. As the taxi took us down to the bus station near the city centre, we passed a group of Indians making their way to the central market. With their bundles of clothes and food over their shoulders, they walked silently, heads bowed towards the cobblestones like hunchbacks. At the bus station some women were propped against the wall, stacking the morning newspapers, and a group of small boys were squatting around a bonfire of street rubbish sharing a paper cup of soup. Long before he had become a guerrilla fighter, when he was still a student doctor, Che had travelled on a motorbike round the poorer regions of northern Argentina, not so far from the Bolivian border. In his diary he recorded a night when he had come across a scene much like this. So moved had he been by the desolation of the peasants that he had clothed an urchin in his jacket. 'Although it was the coldest night of my life,' he had written, 'it was also the warmest moment of my life because for the first time I felt close to the proletariat.' I envied his sense of solidarity that morning in La Paz. All I could think of in the sub-zero temperature was getting into the bus as quickly as possible, to watch the people of the city through a glass window.

We were a small group, bleary-eyed, and grubby from cheap hotels. There was an English agronomist called Peter, who sat smoking a pipe, and near him an Italian couple who looked around nervously. They both seemed to be desperate to go to the lavatory, but the bus didn't have one. Eventually the woman leapt to her feet and left the bus, followed closely by her male companion. I could see them through the window, going up to the newspaper women, asking each one in turn for directions, and getting either a blank look or nod in response. When they reached the bonfire, one of the urchins pointed to the rubbish and then burst out laughing. The Italians went on walking down the street until they simultaneously pulled down their trousers and shat on the pavement.

We travelled for about two hours along a very straight and empty highway. On the way we stopped off at the ruins of Tiahuanaco, dating from AD 800, where an Indian followed us around the ancient blocks of stone, offering to sell us a bronze miniature of an Inca god. Then the concrete softened and the grass turned greener, and we glimpsed a herd of llamas making their way down to the shore of Lake Titicaca.

It was difficult not to feel overawed by this mass of inland sea, the 'highest navigable water' on earth, which stretched out across the plateau as far as the eye could see. Thousands of years before Christ Indians had lived here. Whole generations had been wiped out by great floods but other generations had followed. Creation had been reassembled in the upper limits. New tribes had come with the same traditions, and now the Indians we saw fishing on the turquoise waters in their canoes made of reeds seemed the personification of old stone carvings. Not much is known about the lake's early history, although its identity is believed to have been consolidated by the Incas, the 'people of the sun'. Titicaca means the 'shape of the tiger'. It was named that thousands, perhaps millions of years ago, but the white man discovered the reason thanks to Skylab, the US satellite. As it revolved over South America, Skylab took pictures of the lake, encircled by land, which showed that it was the shape of a tiger. Just how the Indians in their canoes managed to identify the shape of Titicaca remains a mystery.

We crossed the lake, in a small steam boat, thinking on history and legend. It was raining again, with huge hailstones puncturing the grey water like shrapnel. Then the air cleared and the sun turned the lake into a floating tapestry of mixed colours and shades. We made a brief stopover at a small island which, according to Inca tradition, marked the spot where the sun god had left his two children with the mission to teach humanity. Garcilaso de la Vega tells how the Indians complemented this fable with another. This was that the rays of the sun touched the island before any other part of the world after the flood. It was because of these fables, that the Island of the Sun came to be regarded in early history as the 'centre of the Inca Empire'. The Empire we encountered had been reduced to a small mass of sandy soil overhung with eucalyptus, above which there was a maze and some stone ruins. To get to them, we had to run a gauntlet formed by little Indian girls who wanted to sell us coloured ribbons and toy boats. 'Buy me . . . photograph me,' the girls cried in unison. One of them broke from the main pack and came up to me. She could not have been more than about thirteen years old, but she was carrying a small baby wrapped in a bundle on her back. She asked if I had a biro I could give her so that she could learn to write. We had read in an American guidebook that it was advisable to travel round Bolivia well stocked with biros because coins were in themselves worthless and to be charitable with notes would mean having to transport a lorryload of pesos. So I had at that moment about thirty biros in my handbag. I gave all thirty to the girl, leaving her to work out the distribution as we plodded up the ancient steps of the sun kings.

The boat left us eventually on the shores of Copacabana, a different scene from its namesake in Rio. It was a small town of red-roofed houses seemingly carved out of a canyon. 'The region of Lake Titicaca', the boatman had said, 'not only has every kind of weather, but is also filled with rich natural resources. There is nothing you cannot grow here.' But there seemed to be a lot you couldn't grow in Copacabana. Three Indians walking up from the lake had sacks filled only with shrivelled potatoes, and the one vegetable patch I saw was covered in unruly weed and flooded. Overlooking the village was a steep ridge, bare except for some crosses where the local Catholics did their penance. The only other human exercise was being performed at a local army camp, which was perched on the edge of the water. When we arrived there was a small regiment of conscripts, their heads shaved and wearing some ill-fitting fatigues, being screamed at by a Sergeant as they marched backwards and forwards along a wooden jetty. It was not hard to believe that Bolivia had had almost as many military governments as England had Kings and Queens.

For lunch we made our way to the Blue Beach Hotel – the only public house in the village offering board and accommodation, although no hot water – where Peter had a fracas with a waiter called Simón. 'You're charging me for the drink but this says meal and drink all inclusive,' said Peter in broken Spanish as he waved a book of coupons similar to the ones I'd seen Roxanne handing out on the evening of folklore in La Paz. What Peter could have said is what he had told us on the bus, that he had left his pesos behind so as not to be overburdened once he had reached the border with Peru, where he intended to be that evening.

'You pay or you get arrested,' said Simón, a little dark man with protruding yellow teeth which sneered. 'You must remember this is not your country, this is Bolivia. Bolivia,' he repeated as if the point had not found its mark sufficiently.

It ended with me paying Simón and Peter withdrawing rather sheepishly to our table. Peter knew we weren't going on towards Peru on this trip so he gave us an address in Buckinghamshire and promised he would pay us back when we'd got back to England. I privately hoped never to come across him again, not even in Buckinghamshire.

Simón suggested we should come back for supper. Peter pressed on towards Peru and Kidge and I had a meal in the only bar we could find that night in Copacabana. We sat in a narrow damp corridor filled with squat wooden tables, beneath a 1950s poster of a blonde girl advertising some toothpaste. The Indians who sat next to us sharing the dish of the day – roast mutton with potatoes – chewed and burped and had few teeth.

Afterwards, Simón was waiting for us. 'So my supper no good enough for you *Ingleses*,' he said as he handed us our room key. I could have said we had had no supper, that we had simply gone for a long walk along the shores of Lake Titicaca. But it was pouring with rain again and we were dry and stinking of garlic so I thought it best to say nothing. That night we went to bed inspired by a pair of cats copulating on the roof. Later I had a dream that Simón was the Inca god on the Island of the Sun and that at his feet the little urchin girls danced to the tune of a brass band with ribbons and biros, before our boat sank and we were eaten by tigers beneath the waters of Lake Titicaca.

Sucre, the 'official capital of Bolivia', was asleep when we entered it early one afternoon. We had caught a bus back to La Paz and from there a plane. In normal circumstances, the trip should not have taken more than four hours, but there never seemed to be 'normal circumstances' in Bolivia unless normality meant a country in which no one ever seemed to be telling the truth, and where nothing ran on time. Now there were always strikes in Bolivia when at an earlier stage in its history there had been coups. My diary went blank for a while in Bolivia because I was dulled by waiting in airports for planes that didn't exist. In Sucre, at least, there seemed no need to worry about delays or punctuality. Time in this old colonial capital of generous *plazas* and whitewashed 'government buildings' had stopped still.

Sucre's beautiful seventeenth-century cathedral had clearly been reserved for the very pious and dutiful. It was open to the public only from 7.30 to 9.30 in the morning. Presumably for the rest of the day and night only ghosts prayed there. I wanted to meet them. As a child in Spain I had learnt that the most impregnable of churches had a little side entrance by which the priest or his housekeeper could sneak in and out without anyone noticing. So finding the main wooden doors to the cathedral firmly locked, I looked for an entrance down a narrow side street, which was empty except for a donkey chained to a wall. Near the animal an open iron gate gave on to a small courtyard, illuminated by the sun, and beyond this was a door to a small room backed up against the side of the cathedral. In the courtyard were two very blond and very dirty little boys. They had nothing on except for yellowish underpants, and were sleeping on the stone floor where the sun had cast a shadow. It was there the mysteries of Sucre cathedral were revealed to us thanks to the good offices of their father, Juan Imbécil or John the halfwit.

Juan was cross-eyed, spoke with a stutter, and dragged his right foot. He had a nervous tic which occasionally jerked his head and enlarged his eyes, transforming him horribly. It was impossible to ignore him as he took us round the dark interior of the cathedral, hundreds of keys jangling by his side, the two little urchins shuffling and tripping over each other not so far behind. As we walked down a side aisle, lined with saints and candles, Juan said to me in ungrammatical Spanish, in the midst of one of his nervous tics, 'Italiano dos años atrás todo robó . . . no poder . . . ventana se cerró y se cagó . . . ' (Italian two years ago stole everything . . . couldn't . . . window shut and he was buggered.)

'Robó qué?' I asked.

Juan said not a word but instead quickened his pace a little and waved to us to keep up with him. He led us to a side chapel. It smelt of incense and was filled with hundreds of burnt-out candles, but the altar was undistinguished except for a semi-circular metal container that rested on it. Juan told us to sit down. We sat on a wooden bench. Then the little light in the chapel was turned off.

'Now, you see,' said Juan as the children giggled. A spotlight was switched on and focused on the metal container. As its doors revolved, activated by a hidden mechanism, the Virgin of Guadalupe made her appearance. She was a small woman, as small as a cardboard doll. Both her figure and face were buried in a dress encrusted with pearls and emeralds. The chapel had been electrified with 90,000 precious stones.

Right:
The grandmother
Below:
Graffiti,
Santa Cruz,
Bolivia

Above: Christmas disguise, Plaza de Independencia, Quito
Below: Market day, Central Ecuador

Above: Otovalo Indians *Below:* The great divide

Right:
A Colorado
Indian
Below:
Andean family

The municipal band, Cuzco

Above: Epiphany in Cuzco
Right: 'You want a photograph, you pay ten dollars'

Above: Kidge on the train to Machu Picchu *Below:* Machu Picchu

'Madre Misercordia,' said Juan. He was by the altar, and for the first time since we had met he was standing upright, crossing himself.

Juan took us next to the cathedral vestry where normally visits were by strict appointment with the Padre Tesorero only. Encased in glass were a priceless monstrance and other priestly jewels. Next to them was a large wooden cabinet, in which the priest's gold-lined vestments had been laid out. Juan unfurled them in silence and with minimum ceremony, like a mother airing her children's clothes. 'Padre Tesorero . . . mucho oro tiene,' ('Father Treasurer . . . much gold he has') said Juan.

When I asked him where it came from, he said, 'Eldorado.' The children giggled.

Hanging from one side of the cabinet was a bunch of keys the size of hammers. Juan told us that these were the keys to the front doors of the cathedral which were used only if *el Señor Presidente* came. He stood back and shook them in front of the children. The two boys screeched simultaneously and ran out of the room. Juan's head grew and his eyes enlarged. 'Llaves de San Pedro son . . . para llegar al cielo necesitamos,' ('Keys of Saint Peter they are . . . to get to heaven we need them') he said.

We left through the patio, where the two boys were sleeping again. Juan bowed his head as he took our money, waited for us to step out on to the street, then closed the gates and locked them.

We walked across the plaza, up a hill, and towards the tourist office in search of a way of getting to Potosí by nightfall. The tourist office, like most of the town, was still closed and a policeman standing at its doors told us that the road to Potosí was covered in water and was impossible to drive on until the following month when the rainy season had begun to clear. He said there was a plane leaving for Potosí from Lake Titicaca in four days' time, but the national airline was on strike. 'What about the train?' I asked. The train wasn't going any-where, the policeman said, because the engine had broken down and La Paz couldn't find a replacement. He suggested we go back to La Paz and come back later. 'Although you could try Walter. He likes walking on water,' he said pointing up the hill to where Walter was sleeping on the pavement by his bright red old Peugeot . . .

'I don't know if the river is covered with water, but if it is we'll cross it,' said Walter when we had woken him. He was very fat and had a pair of bloodshot eyes set deep into a forest of thick eyebrows.

He smelt very strongly of garlic. Although I had read that Potosí was only a four-hour drive away, Walter prepared his car as if we were about to set out on a much longer journey. He packed in several sleeping bags, two spare wheels, a demijohn of wine, and a tank of spare petrol.

Walter drove us through a valley and across a range of hills, over landscape covered in golden earth and rivulets that glistened in the sun, up and down and over like a helter skelter. On the way to Potosí we skidded and bumped our way through five streams but in the sixth we got stuck. At first Walter held firm, pressing on the accelerator, changing gears, and spinning the steering wheel from one side to the other. But we soon began to feel the car sinking into mud and heard the exhaust splutter water like an outboard engine.

'We need help,' said Walter, his face displaying nervous concern for the first time on the trip. No sooner had he said this than we caught sight of two Indian labourers walking behind a donkey on the other bank of the river. The three of us shouted and waved frantically. The Indians stopped, looked in our direction and then appeared to argue. As one of them began walking down towards us, the other walked on with his donkey.

The skin of the Indian who approached us was textured like the landscape. He wore a woollen cap and a poncho of coarse wool, and seemed to be regurgitating some coca leaves. He was skinny and small but soon demonstrated herculean strength. Without saying a word, he spent the next half-hour picking small rocks from one side of the river and dropping them on the other until he had built up a dam capable of altering the direction of the water. Soon the water drained from under the car. The wheels were still sunk deep, but Walter and the Indian put two large bits of wood across the front and back and the car was released.

The Indian took our money and our cigarettes and walked back towards the hills. Dusk was turning the landscape into the shapes of dark monsters, indistinguishable from the bulbous patches of cloud. And when night finally fell, we gaped out of the windows of Walter's car. The sky was a brilliant canopy of stars – multiplied a millionfold and seemingly raining planets over the land.

In Potosí, if you fell asleep, you were most likely to get killed. It was the place where Spaniards had first discovered silver in 1545 and ever since then Potosí had been a mining town where it was not wise to lose your concentration. This was the sixteenth-century's Big Bang, when an Indian village was exploited for all its physical and mineral worth, becoming the biggest town in the southern hemisphere in just fifty years with a population of 150,000. For South America, the history of money began and ended here in this rugged mountain enclave, five hundred kilometres south of La Paz, where the Spaniards found so much silver they came to boast they could build a bridge of it all the way from Sucre to Madrid. The streets with the palaces and grand mansions recalled past glories, but there were places too that served as a lasting reminder of the hardship and exploitation. In the Casa de la Moneda or Royal Mint the stone floors had been eroded by the naked feet of slaves.

Thanks to Roxanne and Walter, we had followed the trail of Francisco Pizarro, a pig rearer who in the sixteenth century defeated the remnants of the Inca Empire of Lake Titicaca before moving south, along the Altiplano, to gorge himself on the silver of Potosí. But in Potosí now the silver was restricted to museums, and the population was 25,000 less than it had been four hundred years ago. To go down the mine had become a tourist attraction like the Chamber of Horrors at Madame Tussaud's, only the miners here still had to work to live, and to die.

After spending a night in a colonial mansion which had been converted into a hotel, we were picked up by Walter and taken up to the Cerro Rico, Potosí's 'rich mountain' which now produced tin, a commodity which decorates no one but without which there would be no canned food. The change of product had not changed the miners' lot. Along the way we passed the company 'village': a poorly lit compound of pale huts, ringed by an outer wall. It looked like a concentration camp. Beyond it lay the Cerro with its multi-coloured faces, where different minerals had been excavated. Miners were arriving in trucks, huddled together like cattle. They stepped on to small trams and disappeared down the tunnel. These were the day-shift workers who saw the light of day only momentarily. In 1952 the miners of Bolivia had been the principal force behind the country's radical change of government, which had brought about the national-isation of the mines and the acknowledgement of the men who worked as a central and honourable part of society. But the men we saw were silent and subdued, ordered about by managers and photographed by tourists. This generation had been broken politically by a succession of right-wing governments. 'Those who fight are never heard, but most of us are too scared or indifferent to even fight. We merely exist,' said Francisco, a friend of Walter's who had offered to take us into the mine.

Francisco was an ex-miner himself, prematurely retired through ill-health. When he talked, each sentence was accompanied by a cough and a splutter, and he walked with a limp. He looked much older than his forty-five years. He told us that he had gone down the mine for the first time at the age of eighteen. It was his legs that had gone first – a combination of rheumatism from the damp and crushing by falling rocks. Then his lungs had begun to suffer. He had contracted the miners' disease called silicosis.

'There is perhaps no more accurate way of describing a Bolivian mine than as a living hell,' said Francisco, his eyes watering as he fought off his first coughing fit of the day. 'In Potosí there is a popular saying that God graces the town with thirty churches but the devil laughs in its three thousand mines.' The devil was reclining on a cardboard box facing the central mine shaft. He was naked except for a piece of blue and white crêpe paper which was gathered round his horns and tumbled on to his body. He was made of terracotta, but Francisco acknowledged him like an old friend by placing a lighted cigarette between his bright red lips. The devil smiled back mischievously. 'He's my *tío*. Maybe he'll bring us good luck. Maybe he'll spit it out to laugh as the walls collapse on us,' said Francisco.

It was not long before I began to think about Francisco's *tío*. We had walked about two hundred yards when the tunnel narrowed suddenly and we lost sight of the entrance. We were now totally dependent on the carbide lights we were holding to stop our heads from cracking against the wooden beams that provided only token resistance to the rock. We groped our way through an increasingly narrow passageway where the air was thick with dust. The light from our lamps reflected the *tíos* on the stone as Francisco now coughed almost continuously, his anguished breathing echoing through the mine. Francisco told us we were at level two, about a mile and a half down one of the higher levels of the mine. At level three we caught a glimpse of some miners stripped to their underpants repairing a beam. The air was suffocating as we crawled in single file to the edge of the main lift shaft. We heard a clanking of chains and several voices up above us, and then a metal box filled with miners passed us on the way down. Here was one of the main accident points of Cerro Rico.

When the chains broke – as they often did – men and minerals scattered down the shaft like so many bits of discarded rubbish.

Francisco told us that the men in the lift were going down to level five, where the main mining work was going on with pickaxes, drills and shovels. 'The company won't let you go down there. They say the miners don't want to be part of a tourist spectacle. But the truth is that if you didn't die you'd come away denouncing to the world that teenagers were still working as slaves,' said Francisco. Even if I hadn't been able to imagine the slaves, working in the heat and staleness of the middle of the mountain at the centre of the earth, Francisco would not have allowed me to forget.

He took us to what he called his 'hospital'. It was back on level two, a small first-aid room in a cavern stripped of its minerals many years before. In the narrow space there was a small wooden table covered with medicine bottles and syringes and a cigar box filled with white pills. 'Here, take one of these aspirin, it will stop your head throbbing,' he said. I noticed that propped up against one of the bottles was a picture of the Virgin of Guadalupe. I asked him who was important down the mine, the *tío* or the Virgin. He said they were both as important as each other.

Sitting there in his hospital, Francisco told us about the life of the miners. He talked of them as if they were condemned men in a high security prison. They were paid an average wage of thirty dollars a month for a forty-eight-hour week. 'If they do not suffer or die in an accident in the first two years, they contract silicosis in the next two,' he said. He reeled off the statistics like tombstones: five minor accidents per day . . . fifteen 'serious' ones per month . . . an average of forty deaths per year . . . He told us that those killed after blasting with dynamite were buried like worms in a mass of dust and stone. The lucky ones were knocked unconscious never to revive, but most suffered a slow and tortured death by suffocation. The dead and buried usually lay where they fell for two or three days, their broken bodies decomposing rapidly in the heat, before the rescue team arrived.

As we walked back with Francisco, I thought of the silver and the zinc, the lead and the tin that came out of the mines of Bolivia. In another part of the world, many thousands of miles from here, the manufactured product was being sold and resold, picked up in supermarkets by bored housewives, traded and speculated on by clear-lunged commodity brokers, and eventually what was hacked at in the

Cerro Rico found itself on display in jewellers or packaging baked beans. At the entrance to the tunnel, Francisco's *tío* had smoked his cigarette and was grinning still.

— 6 —

RED INDIANS

On a plane bound for Quito, the capital of Ecuador, we sat next to Bill Lyn, who claimed to be a former bodyguard of Elvis Presley. He began the journey with a pair of headphones on, holding a sheet of paper and tapping his feet against the plastic leg of the seat in front of him. The piece of paper had 'King Creole', one of Elvis's songs, neatly typed on it like a hymn. When the song had finished, Bill took his headphones off, began talking, and hardly stopped till we reached Quito three hours later.

Bill didn't begin by telling me about Elvis. He described himself first as a 'night club impresario'. He had spent the previous few months travelling round South America, looking for suitable sites. He had just been in Colombia. 'In Bogotá you can make a lot of money, but the minute you do it gets ripped off or your place gets torn apart. That's what drugs do to a country,' he said. 'Personally, I think Montevideo is my favourite town. It's the safest place politically on the continent, and the US Embassy gives me a hand there.'

I told Bill about a recent trip I had made to Montevideo when the military was still in power. The riot police had broken up a demonstration and an American journalist and I had been arrested. I said I was very scared when they took us down a street without lights in the middle of the night and threatened to shoot us against a wall. For in Uruguay the military had made torture a way of life.

'Well, buddie, I hope they sure taught you a lesson. Don't go mixing with communists,' he said. I noticed he had a big ring on his finger. Somehow I thought it was best not to get into a political discussion with Bill so I said, 'Yes, I guess you're right. Tell me, have you always been a night club impresario?'

The story of Bill Lyn's life was contained in a cutting he had taken from a Colombian newspaper which had given full coverage to his recent search for a night club in Bogotá. The newspaper had printed a series of photographs – Bill, much younger, and with his black head greased back rocker-style, sitting behind a set of drums; Bill with his moustache trimmed and his hair neatly combed, Clark Gable style, standing by a swimming pool next to a Hollywood starlet; Bill in a leather jacket, looking like a lumberjack, behind Elvis; then there was Elvis without Bill, gyrating at an angle, holding a microphone with his lips. Bill's finger had wandered across the newspaper and now rested on the photograph of Elvis, tapping and stroking it in turn. 'Everyone says Elvis died of drugs, but that just ain't true. He just died of boredom,' he said, gazing at the photograph.

Bill told me how Elvis had been so bored one night that he had hired a local amusement park so he could have it all to himself as long as he wanted it. Then there were the parties in Bel-Air where he would try and amuse himself with the help of the closed-circuit video system he had secretly installed in all the rooms. Once, the Beatles had visited him during their US tour. According to Bill, John Lennon was immortalised having a pee.

'They've written lots of things about Elvis since he died but they're all untrue. He was kind of a god to me, a real nice guy. You had to get to know him,' Bill said, a lone tear slowly making its way down his right cheek.

The plane's engines revved as we crossed the final stretch of prairie and rose up above the jagged peaks of the Andes.

Bill was still telling me about Elvis when we were approached by a woman with a striking resemblance to Margaret Thatcher. She stood over us, gazing at Bill distractedly.

'I'm terribly sorry to interrupt you, young man, but aren't you . . . you know that marvellous television actor . . . it's the kind of familiar face I never forget,' she said.

'Well actually, ma'm, I never done no plays,' said Bill in his faintly Texan drawl, 'I've been in movies, though . . . '

'Oh, so you've been in films, I just knew you were someone famous.'

'Well, actually, ma'm, I've just been in one movie.'

'Only one film?' she asked in a tone which verged on the edge of disappointment rather than genuine inquiry. 'And what film would that be, young man?'

'I played the drummer in *Heartbreak Blues*,' Bill said pointing to the photograph in his scrapbook. The woman looked at Bill and hiccoughed.

'You know the movie about Elvis falling for the shop broad,' Bill said, his voice turning strangely childlike.

The woman stood blinking at space equidistant between Bill and me. Her eyes then opened wide as she turned to Bill again and gave him a big smile.

'My dear, how very extraordinary . . . just the other day one of my lead players did a marvellous take-off and we had such fun. He got those delightful bottom movements just right.' The woman laughed and Bill, maybe because he hadn't understood a word of her strange language, shook her hand and bowed his head. The plane shuddered as we hit some turbulence.

The woman said, 'Ecuador, here we come. Well, it's been marvellous meeting you . . . if you ever come to Buenos Aires look us up – we're a theatre group called the Suburban Players. My name is Kerr and my daughter is called Deborah – no relation. You Americans pronounce it Car, but that's wrong, of course. Anyway, I hope to see you later.' And with that, she was off. Bill leaned out and watched her walk back down the gangway. He then sat back and with a profound sigh said, 'Now, that's quite a lady. She's English and she's living in Argentina, making movies? I thought you guys had had a war.'

I said, 'Yes, she's something they call an "Anglo-Argentine". Neither English nor Argentine, really.'

The plane had begun to circle the volcanoes and dip down towards Quito – 'Flying into Quito is like falling into a glove,' Bill had said – so I never got round to arguing about the United States and South America or explaining to him why exactly there was a need to excuse people like the Suburban Players.

'Before the Spaniards there were the Incas; before them the Caras; before the Caras a vague people whom they are said to have conquered: and before them? We do not know. Quito does not tell its past or its age. It has the air of remembering more years than it troubles itself to reckon. Yes, Quito is old.'

Thus wrote Blair Niles, an American who visited Ecuador in 1923. Quito had changed greatly or not at all depending where you started. I had read that modern Quito now had fine avenues, and tower-block hotels, and Embassies built like palaces; it was here that Bill Lyn planned one of his future night spots. Kidge and I said goodbye to Bill at the airport and found a *residencia* up a steep and narrow cobbled road where the Quito that the Spaniards had founded had been isolated like a ghetto. Quito here was still as Blair had known it, unchanged and still whispering its past. Two-storey houses built of brick or roughly painted in whitewash or pale blue leant over the narrow sidewalks; the air smelt of herbs and incense and vibrated with the incessant hub of street vendors and urchins tripping over each other, like nervous monkeys in the chaotic jungle of humanity. The poor were safely hidden away here, because the old quarter was well removed from the modern city where the politicians ruled the country and foreigners did business.

By the cathedral – the burial place of Ecuador's nineteenth-century independence hero, General Antonio José de Sucre – a crowd was standing in silence. They were staring at an open cart on which lay the bodies of two boys. They had expressionless black eyes and were naked and very thin and their limbs were twisted and entwined stiffly, like skeletons. Then I saw a piece of protruding flesh, linking them by their sides, and realised that they were Siamese twins. I thought they were dead at first because of the flies that had settled on their faces and the way the crowd looked. But then the twins suddenly jerked, and their teeth started chattering; the cart shook and the flies scattered, and someone came up and put two handkerchiefs in the boys' mouths to stop them from eating their tongues.

The fit of epilepsy lasted for about two minutes and when it finished the flies returned to settle on the white foam that had formed around their mouths. Then each person in the crowd stepped forward and threw a coin into the cart before walking away.

The Blue Lagoon, the *residencia* where we stayed, was in the process of disintegrating. Our room was decorated in yellow-patterned wallpaper that was now peeling at the edges and had a wooden floor with planks that bent under our feet. Its previous occupant had scattered some mango skins about so the place had a sickly sweet smell. In the room next door, separated from us by a thin wall of cardboard, lived a couple of American travellers. There was rarely a moment's silence from them. Radio blaring in early morning, complaints to the hotel maid about the service at lunchtime, and the rattling of bed springs and escalating expressions of passion in the evening. Bob and Carol were from Boston and had been travelling round South America for four months. Over breakfast they read chapters of Paul Theroux's *The Old Patagonia Express*. We usually found ourselves escaping from them.

We had read that the best way to get to know old Quito was to simply walk around its narrow streets. And this we did by starting in the Calle Ronda, one of the oldest streets of all. It had been raining, and now green, bad-smelling rivulets meandered over the cobblestones. The water dripped from the grilled windows and ran down the whitewash, turning it yellowish. The houses had once belonged to Spanish nobles but were now inhabited by the poor of Quito, who washed their clothes in the river and sold Indian garments to tourists. We walked through a narrow doorway and into a covered patio where a group of Indians sat around a table covered with empty beer bottles. The four men looked as if they had drunk themselves senseless. They sat there, saying not a word and staring blankly at the bottles. Only once did one of them move. He walked unsteadily through the patio and out on to the street and urinated on the cobblestones. Then he returned in silence. The only other client of the 'bar' was an old woman who shuffled in, leaning on a walking stick and holding a plastic bag. The boy behind the counter filled it with chicken bones and vegetable peel and then she shuffled out again.

We sat on a wooden bench, dipping bits of stale bread into some earthenware bowls filled with chicken soup which tasted vaguely of fish. 'Makes a change from Father Christmas in Calle Florida,' said Kidge. And then I remembered that this was Christmas week. 'It's time we heard Mass,' I said.

We walked to La Compañía, a sixteenth-century Jesuit church and one of the oldest surviving buildings in South America. Long ago, the church had been decorated in gold to compete with the Indian temples rather than to bring anyone closer to God. Now that the temples had long since been destroyed, all that was left was a baroque exaggeration. On a wall, just by the main entrance, was a huge mural depicting hell. 'Impurity' was personified by a monkey vomiting over a naked Indian and 'adultery' by a wolf biting a woman's nipple. On one side of the main door an impressively carved wooden spiral staircase led up to the choir loft; on the other, a copy of the staircase had been painted on to a mural. There seemed to be no rational explanation for this other than the Jesuits had wanted to keep the whole place symmetrical. 'Maybe they had simply run out of gold,' suggested Kidge.

The Mass had not yet begun. The place was packed with Indians in ponchos and thick woollen hats and yet, to our amazement, we heard over the loudspeakers a tape of Christmas carols sung in English. There was a faithful rendering of 'Silent Night', followed by 'Away in a Manger'. Then the tape suddenly cut and on came a high-pitched American girl's voice asking Father Christmas for her two front teeth.

The congregation murmured, coughed and spat. Hanging heavily in the air was the, by now familiar, Quito smell of stale cheese and urine. This became particularly intense when a large woman with billowing skirts came and sat herself along the bench from us. She had a baby sucking from a very large breast, and a two year old leaning against her legs breaking the shell of an egg. As he bit into it, the egg let off a strong smell of sulphur.

The priest who eventually celebrated Mass had a head that was egg-shaped. It peeped out from a huge gold-lined chasuble. He gave a sermon about the humanity of the Christmas story which everyone listened to attentively.

Afterwards we walked out into an old street, unchanged from the days of the *conquistadores*, and caught the brilliant mid-morning light. With a reflected radiance, Kidge turned and with a smile said, 'Happy Christmas.'

It was the Christmas that the IRA detonated a bomb outside Harrods. In Quito, the Indians were doing good business with their cartloads along the Avenida 24 de Mayo; cartloads filled with every junk item imaginable from impossibly sized plastic shoes to garish portraits of Jesus Christ, all bright browns and tinsel borders. There was an electric train which would always go only half round the track before getting derailed, bags of herbs and trays of chewing gum, and a whistle that made the sound of an Andean bird. In the large Plaza de Independencia, in front of the cathedral, an Indian sat disguised as Father Christmas. Two children perched on his lap, bawling their heads off, as if they'd just been chosen for sacrifice. Near him, some urchins were letting off firework crackers and a clown was dancing a jig holding an open box filled with coins. 'Remember, you can give only as much as you're given,' said the clown, his painted face set in the most melancholic of smiles. On the cathedral steps, the crippled and insane of the city had taken up their positions – a litany of rattling limbs and empty tins, high-pitched screeches and monologues. After a while they were joined by an old man pushing a cart. I walked over to him and recognised the Siamese twins.

'Are they dead?' I asked.

'No, just dying,' the old man said.

'But is there nothing one can do?' I insisted.

'Nothing. They have the devil inside.'

And then I realised that here in the Plaza de Independencia I had come the closest I had ever been to that transitional resting place of human souls Catholics call limbo. No one was going backwards or forwards in this place of oblivion, with sideshows not even the protagonists meant to happen. And the IRA and Harrods belonged to another planet to that we found ourselves in now. Near the edge of the highest volcano in the world, just a few miles from the equator, we had landed in the most remote of South American capitals.

We left Quito on Boxing Day on a bus that played 'Jingle Bells' over its loudspeakers on a route that would take us eventually to the Pacific coast. The bus was an antique, with wooden seats and iron bars to steady yourself on. It was soon filled with Indians holding live chickens and bundles of potatoes between their legs. As the engine began revving, a late arrival stumbled into the bus and made her way down the gangway. She was a white Ecuadorian, jewelled and wearing a fur coat and heavily scented. She was clutching two large leather suitcases and a bright red velvet hatbox. She looked like an opera singer on the run. I watched her wade through the crowded bus before tripping on a chicken and collapsing rather ungraciously into the only remaining empty seat. 'This bus smells of cheese,' she said. They were the only words she uttered in the whole journey.

The road twisted and turned through a spectacular mix of scenery ranging from high, arid mountain peaks to huge fertile valleys covered in lush vegetation. The first stage of the route was lined with children kneeling and begging for food from the passing traffic. But we hardly noticed them, so concerned were we about our own survival. The driver sat perched high above us all. He kept one hand on the steering wheel and the other in a permanent state of anarchic gesticulation. Whenever we approached a hairpin bend, he raised the pitch of the argument with his co-driver so the bus usually turned the corner with its nose pointing towards an abyss. Their conversation revolved around the range of speeds that our particular bus was capable of doing at any given moment. For much of the time the gears stuck in neutral, leaving us in the hands of fortune as the bus freewheeled its way down the mountain.

Beside me, Francisco, a young *mestizo* doctor with a thin moustache and aquiline nose, told me that Ecuador had been falling apart since the recent death of the popular presidential candidate. 'Roldos was the only decent politician we've ever had before they killed him. It's been downhill since then. Growing bananas that's all we're good for and who wants bananas anyway? All that sugar and water . . . makes you fat.'

Along the gangway, the chicken which had earlier tripped up the woman in the fur coat, had escaped from between its owner's legs again and was clucking and screeching its way in and out of the seats. It was throwing feathers in the air and when it came to where we were sitting squirted some shit on the doctor's shoes.

Francisco said, 'You see Ecuador is like a chicken on the loose. No one controls it and it shits.'

I asked him why he had left Quito. 'Everyone is drunk all the time and no one cares. I can't take that kind of *modus vivendi*.'

We had planned to stay on the bus for the five-hour journey to the Pacific coast, but when Francisco said he was also going there we decided to get off at the earliest opportunity. In this part of the world I had hoped that doctors would be like good priests, sharing the burdens of an unjust society with an unflagging trust in change. But Francisco was a cynic.

We passed the tangled metal frame of a bus on the edge of the mountain where, according to Francisco, there had been an accident just two days earlier. 'The driver was so drunk he thought he was an airline pilot. Everyone got killed. Serves them right.' And then we freewheeled downwards again. The road now had banana trees along its side and the air was denser, more sweet-smelling than it had been in Quito. We were approaching a crossroads where an Indian woman was dragging a black pig on the end of a long rope. As we came nearer the pig ran ahead of the woman, catching her legs with the rope and making her fall on the ground. She only just managed to get up in time to wave to the bus to stop for her.

We left Francisco as he started another diatribe against the pigs of the land. His shouts and the screeching of the pig were audible above the rattling of the engine; then the bus bumped and shook its way down the hill and disappeared round a corner in a cloud of dust. When it had gone, it was as if a great peace had taken hold of us. Above the road the land, sandy and cracked, rose through a wood of conifers which was filled with birdsong and the reverberations of insects. A signpost announced the town of Santo Domingo was three kilometres away, and another in smaller lettering pointed to Tinalandia. We followed the direction of the second through a clearing in the wood, along a path lined with wild flowers. All around, giant multi-coloured butterflies hovered and danced, their wings flapping in broad strokes like fans. It was late afternoon so the sun's rays cut through the forest at angles, sharpening the colours of the foliage. The first evidence of human life we came across was a large wooden bandstand. Cobwebs the size of trampolines were entwined between its pillars and part of the wood was cracked and rotting. It seemed that no orchestra had played there for about fifty years. Near it were some wooden huts on stilts and beyond a larger house with some signs of human life within.

'Looking for a room?' someone said.

We turned and saw a man in riding breeches and open white shirt, holding a whip in one hand and a cigar in the other. He cut a striking figure, there on the edge of the tropics, on that December afternoon. He was tall and broad shouldered, and had a strong, handsome, if deeply lined face that defied any precise estimate of age beyond fifty.

I said we would take a room and some supper if there was any available.

'My son, in Tinalandia if nothing is available we shall try and find it for you.'

As we walked towards the house, the man swatted at the butterflies and took long pulls on his cigar. Then he came to attention at the entrance to the house, and clicked his heels like a storm trooper.

'Allow me to introduce myself. My name is Alfredo. I am the husband of the lady of this house, Tina, the Duchess of Platinov. I shall leave you now.' And with that he turned, bowed and marched off back towards the forest, leaving a trail of dead butterflies behind him.

In the hall of the hotel, three maids standing in a row curtsied as we walked in. They were dressed in black and with white aprons. One of them asked us to fill in the visitors' book while her two companions ran off into a distant kitchen. We were seated at one end of a long, empty, wooden table, laid for four. The room was poorly lit with oil lamps, but I could make out some low beams and a couple of old portraits over an open fireplace. One of them was of Alfredo as a young man, dressed in military uniform. The other, a woman with a high neck and firm cheekbones and stunning blue eyes, I assumed was Tina Platinov, also many years before. But the most striking feature of the room was an open veranda through which we saw the day quickly fade and night fall with a pervading sense of unreality. With the darkness, the forest became filled with the sounds of frogs and crickets and the whooping of night birds; then came the insects. The bats were the first to swoop in on us, followed closely by the giant moths. They gathered on the veranda in bundles, casting demonic shadows across the room. Kidge was sitting, drinking some Coke, when one of the moths detached itself, flew haphazardly over the table, and landed in her glass. Its wings were so large that when they flapped, in an effort to escape, they knocked the glass over. Next we heard a faint crackle from the opposite end of the table and saw a black object climb over the rim of a plate and gradually move towards us. As it came nearer we saw that it was a giant cockroach, as black and large as the moth but more sinister. Its skin glistened, and as it dragged itself across the table it left a sulphurous-smelling trail of liquid behind it.

'Don't worry, it won't bite you. It may look naughty but it's actually harmless.' Leaning against the doorway stood a short tubby man in tennis shorts and a baseball cap, holding a butterfly net. He walked over and deftly brushed the cockroach off the table as if it had been a breadcrumb. He introduced himself as Sam. He was followed by his friend, Larry, a physical and mental opposite, elongated and brittle where Sam was rounded and boisterous.

They joined us at table, with the moths and the bats committing collective suicide against the windowpane on the veranda, and the cockroaches smearing the stone floor with their insidious progress. And as the maids with their black uniforms and white aprons served us ritualistically a supper of avocados and suckling pig, Sam and Larry told us a little about their lives. Sam had once run an English pub near the British Embassy in Quito. Larry described himself as a former Civil Servant. They had met many years ago on a tea plantation in India. They were now travelling round South America in search of rare insects on commission for a museum of natural history.

Sam said, 'It used to be easy to get anything you like out of this country. But now government officials have realised that even a moth can fetch a price in the developed world. You should see the hassle we have getting these blighters through the customs. The new jargon is that we're "exporting the national heritage".'

I asked him about Tina Platinov, and Sam told the story.

'As the young wife of a White Russian Duke called Platinov she escaped from the Revolution in 1917. She hid in an Italian submarine and ended up in Paris. She was beautiful and charming and very rich – you know, the Greta Garbo type, and she had absolutely no problem settling down in Paris. They simply adored her. Her husband, old

Platinov, was quite awful. Always drunk on vodka and running off with other women. Luckily for Tina he was also fond of duelling. One day the old shit shot his best friend in a duel and was politely asked to leave France rather than face the scandal of a public trial. You could get away with that still in the 1930s. The bait was a large tract of land which the then Ecuadorian government had leased to the French in return for some trade – bananas probably. That's all you get here, bananas and moths, you know. So Platinov took the opportunity to become a man of property again in a country of agricultural serfs. In Ecuador Platinov got older and more unpleasant and the beautiful Tina more restless and naughty. Enter "Rudolph Valentino". Their neighbour was a young broad-shouldered *estanciero* called Alfredo. He soon became Tina's lover. Platinov died of rheumatism and Tina and Alfredo have lived together ever since.'

When Sam had finished, I looked around the room. Over the fireplace, a group of moths had settled over the two portraits, which now stared out at us with an unsettling detachment.

In a few minutes we saw Tina. A tall, thin and very old woman swept into the dining room, dressed in a long silk gown that trailed behind her. She was wearing a broad-brimmed velvet hat and smelt of mothballs. She was bowing to each side as she walked as if acknowledging an invisible line of courtiers and above her head fluttered dozens of brightly coloured moths. She was followed by Alfredo. He walked slowly, staring straight in front of him, his step rigidly marking time as if goose-stepping. Neither of them turned or said a word as they passed us. Instead they went over to the end of the table and sat in silence near to the veranda where the insects were squashing themselves against the windowpane. A few minutes later they rose and left the room. By then the abstraction of the scene had permeated the room and we had taken to lighting each other's cigarettes for reassurance.

Sam held his deftly between his fingers before drawing on it with a long, lascivious suck. 'You know, the natives round here believe that they're living with Tina's second life and that she is a rambling spirit.' I supposed they were right. Here in the tropics time had stopped and the multitude of insects hinted at disorder and the afterlife. At least that is how it seemed in that hotel, where those of us who sat around the table seemed diminished, disconcerted and deluded. I believed that only beyond the building was it possible to reassert a sense of reality, of management.

After supper, Sam and Larry drove us up to their 'camp'. It was up the hill, on the edge of the woods, close to where Alfredo and Tina had built a golf course. We parked by a solitary transit van. Near it there was a bright lamp on a stand shining on to a white sheet which was propped up with stakes and tent pins like a piece of animal skin. Larry walked around it, pulling here, loosening there, stroking the material as he went with the diligence of a good fisherman preparing his nets.

To the sheet were stuck hundreds of moths of every imaginable shape and colour. Sam slowly shone a torch, lingering on the more dramatic ones, which had wings of bright red with an outer border of golden yellow. Then Larry produced from a bag a pair of pincers and a syringe.

'It's ammonia. They don't feel a thing,' he said.

And so Sam went to each moth, injecting it with a small lethal dose before dropping it in a minute paper bag of the kind that stamp collectors use. Down at Tina's the moths had filled the house with spirits. But up here on the hill, the mass annihilation had momentarily reduced them to the inanimate state of dried leaves. Eventually Sam drove us back to the house. As we left the camp I caught my last glimpse of Larry. He was holding a butterfly net as he swooped and skipped between the trees. Reflected again in the light of the bright lamp, his movements now seemed to belong to an inspired elf who had decided to show off to his lover.

We slept within the forest in a wooden hut that was perched somewhat crookedly atop some stilts. From our bed we watched a full moon rise between the palisades of the abandoned bandstand and heard the daytime bird song give way to the eerie sounds of the night creatures. We had read somewhere that pumas, tapirs, armadillos, guinea pigs and porcupines were among the creatures that inhabited these regions. We were kept awake by giant mosquitos which hovered outside the hut before squashing themselves against the wire that covered our window. We listened to the pacing of a four-legged creature on the wooden floor of the veranda, its strange purring, and its brief but threatening scratching against the outside wall. We held each other close beneath a blanket that smelt of damp, wishing the darkness away, longing for the light of day. At one point the wind gathered strength, stirring the trees into a frenzy, and covering the moon in a thin translucent mist. The sky itself was illuminated by white lightning, the thunder rumbled and rain drenched the forest. Only then, when the sounds I had found so threatening before had been soaked and washed down into the centre of the earth, did I dare to get out of bed and look out of the window. In the midst of the storm, I glimpsed a tall thin woman in a trailing gown, running between the trees. I thought it could have been Tina, but she was gone too quickly to be sure.

The next day Alfredo was at the door, immaculate in his khaki suit and clutching a cigar in one hand much as we had first seen him. He said his wife would have liked to join him but she was still sleeping. I could not easily erase the image of the night before, so I asked him if Tina usually took walks in the forest. Alfredo laughed heartily. 'What, walk in the forest with the kind of rain we had last night? You need to be mad to do that.' But then I had never made any specific mention of the rain, let alone the recent storm. So Alfredo was lying or his wife was mad or the truth lay somewhere in the middle.

We rejoined the road where we had earlier abandoned the bus from Quito and walked the few miles that were left to Santo Domingo. Tinalandia had left us with a yearning for escape as much as for some purgative exercise, so we ignored most of the vehicles that offered us a lift and stuck to a determined march. The few pedestrians we passed on the way were pushing oxen, or being pulled by pigs, or shuffled, head almost scraping the road, under the weight of sacks of bananas. Walking uphill they seemed to share none of our enthusiasm for the early morning. As we passed each one I sensed that in their suffering and our elation we momentarily epitomised the conflicting fortunes of this divided continent.

Santo Domingo is a commercial centre, which grew out of nothing on the back of Ecuador's over-priced banana exports, and which has since gone into decline. Were it not for the main highway linking Quito with the Pacific coast, it is doubtful whether the town would now exist. For no one had ever thought of building a bypass and the road still runs through the town, churning out trucks and buses and farm labourers looking for work. Santo Domingo dispirited me with its featurelessness.

It was a feeling which grew in the Café Humboldt, a bar overlooking the main square of the town where we stopped off to have our first coffee of the morning. We shared a table with Elaine, a member of the American Peace Corps, who had spent several months 'bringing water' to the local community. She had planned, prospected, dug and eventually built a well. Once completed, the well had been opened with much pomp and fanfare. The local newspaper sent its one photographer, and then there were men in trim blue suits who claimed to represent the American Embassy. 'It was as if we had brought manna to the desert,' said Elaine, her eyes momentarily glistening.

As we talked I looked out at the plaza. At one end, there were faded palm trees outside the labour exchange, and it was there that hundreds of unemployed young farm labourers were submitting themselves to selection for work like cattle at an auction. I thought of the piles of bananas I had seen rotting by the roadside.

'So, what went wrong?' I asked Elaine.

'Some son of a bitch came one night, poisoned the water and then hacked the well to pieces with a pickaxe.'

'Do you know who did it?'

'The Embassy says it was most likely a group of left-wing terrorists. You see whoever did it brought a big paint brush with them and painted a near-by hut with the words: *Agua Yanqui = Agua Mierda.*'

It was at this precise point, when Elaine grimaced as if to stress the horror of it all, that I heard the unmistakable martial jingle of the BBC World Service. It came from a table in the far end of the café which had been empty when we had first walked in but which was now occupied by the gangling figure of someone I knew immediately to be an Englishman. There was a sepulchral look about him. His knees, visible beneath a pair of baggy blue shorts, seemed to have been screwed on to his legs like door knobs to a cupboard. He was listening to his radio with his right ear close to the speaker and his head leaning heavily on an arm. I asked Elaine if she knew him.

'Know him? It's difficult not to get to know Charlie,' Elaine said with a look that left little doubt about a tested intimacy. 'Santo Domingo wouldn't be the same without him.' And she shouted to him across the room that she was with a couple of fellow English people and to cut that BBC crap that had nothing to say about South America. The man switched off the radio and then walked over to us, clutching the radio under his arm.

'Hello, I'm Charles Harvey. You know I couldn't help overhearing you early on. It's so nice to hear a genuinely English voice. It's like a breath of fresh air, really, like the BBC.' Elaine giggled at this, and Charles blew her a kiss.

He told us that he had once worked in Borneo but now lived on a plantation he owned not far from Tinalandia. He couldn't say quite what had brought him to Ecuador ten years before, other than the weather was not unlike Borneo and that the country had a reputation as another South American country that let foreigners do more or less what they wanted. 'It's so poor, you see, that you only invest a penny and they think you're starting the Marshall plan all over again,' Charles said as Elaine settled somewhat awkwardly on his knobbly knees.

In his first months in Ecuador, things had not turned out quite as he had hoped. 'In point of fact, things turned out quite rottenly. I was made a plantation manager by the biggest landowner in the country with pots of money. So much he didn't know what to do with it. They say he made it on some crooked oil deal or something like that. His workers, of course, hated him. I have always tried to be reasonable, fair, you know try and instil a bit of decency among the natives, but to no avail. The only difference they saw was that the landowner was the bastard while I was simply a bastard *Inglés*. One day the workers came to demand more wages. You know what they did while I checked on the accounts? They started sharpening their *machetes* on a piece of stone.'

When he told me this I realised that Elaine and he had been brought together not so much by any mutual physical attraction but by a shared encounter with local revolt – one whose roots lay deep in Ecuador's popular culture. The plight of the *huasipungo*, or landless peasant, had been immortalised by Ecuador's leading novelist Jorge Icaza more than forty years before, and remained in the country's bestseller lists. But as I watched them gently rocking on a wooden chair in the Café Humboldt that morning I suspected that the gap which separated them from Ecuador was probably as wide as that which divided the moth collectors from the spirits of the rain-soaked forest of Tinalandia.

For the rest of the day, however, Charles made every effort to impress upon me that the peasants' revolt had been an aberration and that it was still possible that South Americans liked Englishmen better than they liked Americans. 'I didn't want to tell you with Elaine here,' he said afterwards as he drove us around the town in a rusty truck smelling of bananas, 'but the worst time I've had in Ecuador is since I bought my own place and decided to be my own boss. There's the wicked wife of this simply awful American neighbour of mine who seems intent on wrecking everything I do. She got her husband to block my road once, and has since taken me to court for alleged banana-crop theft. The problem with the yanks is that they've got this terrible superiority thing about South America. They think they own the place. It was a bit like that in Asia.'

Charles had insisted that we shouldn't leave Santo Domingo without first meeting what he described as the town's *dramatis personae*. 'It might look an awful place, but really Santo Domingo is Ecuador in microcosm,' he said. First on the list of characters was Jaime Saltos, the editor and owner of the local newspaper, *El Oriente*. The man lived where he worked, on the damp ground floor of a nondescript concrete block. To get to it we had to negotiate a complex system of hidden alleyways and iron staircases where dogs picked on rotting fruit and half-naked urchins played football. As we passed a window, a washerwoman bared her breast and suckled a screaming baby.

The offices of *El Oriente* were stuffed with the kind of typewriters and printing presses which featured in early photographs of the newspaper industry. I felt instantly nostalgic at the smell of ink and oil, the sight of the fudged stencil paper scattered on the floor, and the sound of the presses cranking and sighing in a distant room, like an old ship's engine.

Jaime was a small, soft-spoken man who greeted us with solemnity and reverence. From the moment he bowed to me and kissed Kidge's hand nothing I could do or say dissuaded him in any way from his assumption that no British journalist would travel as far as Santo Domingo unless he was on a special mission for Her Majesty's government. Flicking through some copies of *El Oriente*, I was impressed by the forthright attitude it had taken towards local politics. One story exposed a local construction scandal in which several leading businessmen appeared to be implicated. Another denounced the torture of a local student who had been picked up by the police on an alleged charge of shop-lifting.

I told Jaime that in England there seemed to be a lot of local newspapers that wrote about little other than horse-riding events and the homosexuality of the local vicar, and that although ours was a democratic country it was often an offence to write bad things about people of influence, not least about the security forces.

'Ah, but Señor Burns, your newspapers have all the technology. You cannot imagine what a great newspaper *El Oriente* would be if your government agreed to donate us a new printing works.'

I suggested he should write directly to Prince Charles and promised

I would talk to the British Ambassador if and when I got back to Quito.

Charles took us next to see Martín Bueno, owner of a local radio station. Bueno's programmes never delved into the construction business, let alone the local police. Too many people listened to the radio in Santo Domingo because there was a high illiteracy rate. His offices belonged to a different world to Jaime's. Here were stacks of hi-fi equipment, intercoms, plush leather furniture, receptionists looking like failed film actresses – all bright red lipstick and plunging necklines. There was no huffing and puffing here or dirty floorboards, just slick, piped PR consciously designed to make the visitor forget this was Ecuador.

Bueno looked like an affluent Hispanic plucked from New York's West Side. He shimmered in his suit and his teeth were locked in a petrified smile. He was flanked by secretaries with clinging dresses and posters of past and present Presidents. He talked very loudly, gesticulating so as to give added emphasis to every word he spoke. The room was lined with tapes and I imagined that each of them was taken up with recordings not of songs but of the sayings of Martín Bueno. Bueno said, 'What is the most important thing for a society? What is it that people NEED? It needs health, but to have health you need knowledge and to have knowledge you need technical know-how. Technology, Mr Burns, is the answer, and we are proud to say we have that here.'

Before we left, Bueno added that he intended to put his radio to full use in the coming election campaign – 'On the side of progress of course.'

Charles drove us back to the square. The building near to where the local unemployed had been standing was now decked out with flags and posters urging the population to vote. The local labour exchange offices had been temporarily handed over to the government candidate for the period of the campaign. I noticed that many of the men who had earlier asked for work on the plantation were now emerging from the building laden with propaganda. I was not surprised when Charles explained that of the seven candidates competing for the mayorship of Santo Domingo, only one was alleged to be free from corrupt practices. He was a local teacher called José Ferrer. He had converted the parlour of his small house into his campaign headquarters. He had several sons and daughters who were his main supporters. While we talked, they kept coming in and out and receiving last-minute instructions about canvassing. The sons crouched at their father's feet while the daughters sat on his lap, before they were each sent on their way with a sign of the cross marked on their foreheads. For José the campaign had become a holy war waged with a biblical sense of blood loyalty. José rated his chances of winning as '5000–1 against – that's more or less the proportion of my family to the local population.' He predicted that Ecuador was heading inexorably towards the umpteenth military coup of its history. As he talked, José paced round the room, pointing to pictures of ancient battles on his wall and dusting his history books. He spoke wearily, with the restrained passion of someone who has waited much too long to have someone listen to his ideas. 'The others make speeches in the public squares, but what's the point of promising you are going to give free food to 50,000 half-starving children if you know that in this town it's a small miracle to have just one stone laid for the poor?'

Long before the road to Quito had been built, Santo Domingo and the land that surrounded it belonged to the Colorados, an Indian tribe of mysterious origins. They were described in José's history books as part nomadic, part sedentary, with roots dating back to Christ. Some books held that they originated near the coast and moved, in the course of centuries, over the mountains and through the forests to the place of vegetation and flowing streams. Other books said they came from outer Mongolia, or that they were descendants of the Incas. They had barely survived the arrival of the Spaniard. Confusion about the Colorados' origins seemed to go to the heart of the nation's identity crisis. When the white settlers pushed westward from Quito, a familiar pattern of conquest, plunder and expulsion followed closely. In Santo Domingo, the Indians were subjugated, cross-bred, turned into slaves; what had earlier been a tribal settlement now became a commercial crossroads linking the town's one-crop economy with the traders of the capital and the commodity brokers of the European cities. The town rode out one cycle after another, boom and bust, boom and bust, with ultimately less boom than bust. In the process it became socially anaesthetised. Not long before our arrival, the local govern-ment had decreed that the descendants of the Colorados should be given a reserve a few kilometres outside the town. The initiative was taken with a great deal of official publicity about the need to preserve an endangered species, and, in so doing, the essentially white or *mestizo* administration chose to ignore that the Colorados were neither butterflies nor tapirs in danger of extinction as a species but a people who had finally lost their basic right to live in a place of their choosing.

Judging by his old manuscripts and books, José had read a great deal about the Colorados, and yet I knew that he had as good as lost his election when he suggested that the only person who had any real access to the Colorados now was Martín Bueno.

So after saying our farewells to José – and later to Charles, who had a farmers' meeting – we were driven to the reserve by Bueno's son, Fredo. The youth was a younger version of his father. He spoke with a loud and self-conscious American accent and drove his pickup with an affected nervous energy he seemed to have contracted from watching too many movies.

The road was dusty and rocky, the countryside increasingly clustered with useless shrubs on which the odd cow or goat fed. Behind us lay the rain forest of Tinalandia, the rivers and the sweating leaves. I caught a glimpse of Santo Domingo through the truck's side window. The town seemed cut out of colourless cardboard, pasted together haphazardly.

Fredo spoke with a lighted cigarette balancing between his lips. He tuned his radio to a rock channel, adjusted the balance of his stereo speakers, and asked us about the state of rock music in England. I asked him about the state of Ecuador. 'What my country needs is the military. The people are too ignorant. They do not understand politics,' he said. I longed to reach our destination.

Along the road we passed two boys sitting on small scrambler motorbikes. They watched us go by without the slightest trace of surprise or interest. For the first time since arriving in Ecuador I felt like a tourist. At José's house, I had read that the Colorado tribe in its heyday may have numbered well over 40,000. Fredo said, 'There can't be more than about three hundred who keep to their cultural traditions, but that's no problem, I'm about to introduce you to the real thing.'

The ground was now muddy and uneven and the gradient rose steeply. Fredo locked his pickup into superdrive, but the vehicle slithered and spun on itself before sliding backwards. Fredo tried again, accelerating harder this time, but now the vehicle slid sideways. We made it on our fourth attempt by taking the one approach up the hill that seemed to be dry. At the top, motionless and with his head slightly tilted to the sky was a Colorado. He had deep red stripes painted on his face and chest. His hair was bound together with a thick paste, and his hands and ears were covered in jewellery. The decoration emphasised rather than obscured his age. The painted body was that of an old and withered man.

No sooner had we stepped out of the truck than the Indian walked a few yards to the side and stood stiffly against a bush of wild roses. 'You can take his picture now,' said Fredo. A few seconds later I was looking through my lens at a small house made of reeds that I had noticed behind the bush. I was about to take a photograph when from behind the hut's doorway peeped the face of a small girl. Her hair was long and tangled, her face a chaos of pock marks and dirt. She pulled a face at me, pushed a finger up her nose, before taking it out and licking it. 'Get out of the way,' I heard Fredo cry to the little girl from behind me. The Indian turned. I clicked.

I asked the Indian about his reserve, but he simply nodded his head. We left soon afterwards. As we stepped into the truck I glimpsed Fredo handing the Indian a thick envelope and talking in lowered voice.

'Is he the Indian chief?' Kidge asked, when Fredo had taken the wheel again.

'No, just a good friend of my father. Now we'll go and see the chief.'

Fredo drove us for about a mile before braking suddenly when the track ended on the edge of a ravine. Below, flowed the first river we had seen in Ecuador. It was wide and turbulent, its waters breaking against the stones and throwing up foam. The air was clear and smelt of wild herbs. I was suddenly gripped with a longing to be rid of Fredo with his dangling cigarette and his faint smell of aftershave. So it was an enormous relief when Fredo said he wanted to sleep in the truck while we visited the chief. We left him reclining on the bonnet of the pickup and crossed the river on a narrow footbridge that lay precariously suspended by ropes on either side. The bridge swung and jerked with our movements and for moments even the sound of the river was blotted out by fear.

On the other side the ground was sodden and pungent, much of it sewage. Two small mounds of earth heaved, rose and then erupted, before materialising into pigs. Their faces were caked with mud, and their bodies had absorbed the oily green of the sewage. The two pigs grunted as they saw us before pushing past and going down towards the river. Beyond the bank, the mud gave way to dust again and a small wood had been cleared to make way for the chief's village. This consisted of a few reed huts interspersed with cabbage patches.

On these, Indians with long black hair tied in pigtails and dressed in long baggy trousers were bent double picking potatoes. Next to them a group of women wearing gold-plated snakes around their necks were weaving on wooden looms. We recognised them as Indians from Otavalo, a township to the north of Quito we had visited briefly during our stay in the capital. In Otavalo they belonged to no one but themselves, proudly showing off and making a living from their elaborate jewellery and embroideries. But here on the edge of the river, the Otavalo Indians worked as cheap migrant labour for the Colorados. The situation was as much a consequence of the development of a local market economy as of the divide and rule policy towards the tribes white Ecuadorians had inherited from the Spaniards.

The chief's lodgings were five huts rolled into one. In the context of the village, such an extension was more distinctive than a palace in a city. The huts were elevated above the rest by thick wooden stilts and their balustrades covered in wild ivy. The Otavalo Indians did not look up when we passed them to climb the staircase that led on to the veranda. There we were met by a woman who seemed to have tried to eradicate whatever trace of Indian she might have once had in her. She had partly bleached blonde hair and thick make-up and wore a tweed skirt quite ill-suited to the tropical heat. 'I am the chief's mother-in-law. Come with me,' the woman said, and we followed her like a pair of curious children. She led us into a large room, where she no longer seemed such a curiosity. It was furnished with a small library of Spanish dictionaries, imitation leather armchairs, garishly designed wallpaper, and a life-size plastic pink elephant. Instead of tables, there were machines: a hi-fi set, a television, a freezer and a washing machine on which rested family photographs and a picture of the Virgin Mary. The woman pointed to an insipid-looking Indian youth on the day of his wedding to a white girl and said that he was the chief. The next minute, Nicanor Calazacón walked in. The pimpled face and unformed adolescent frame was much the same as in the photograph. Only his hair and clothing had changed. His hair was stuck together in the reddish paste the Colorados use as war paint, and instead of a white suit he was dressed in a sweatshirt and pair of jeans. Nicanor looked like someone trapped in the half-way stage of metamorphosis.

Nicanor shook our hands solemnly and without saying a word walked across the room and sat on the pink elephant.

I asked Nicanor how he had become chief of one of the oldest tribes in Ecuador. He told me that his father had died two years before. 'The title should have passed on to the eldest son, but my brother was a drunk and anti-Ecuadorian and it was decreed that I should be voted chief.'

'Who decreed it?' I asked.

'The government, of course,' Nicanor said, looking somewhat startled that I should even think of asking such a question. I wanted Nicanor to explain how it was that an election could be 'decreed' and how a community where illiteracy was widespread could vote anyway, but I thought it more prudent to say simply that I thought the reserve belonged to his people.

'Oh, but it does. I am constantly pressing the authorities to build more roads so we can be more closely linked to Santo Domingo. We are already building a school. We have cleared the forest and a church is being built. There will be carols at Christmas and processions . . . '

. . . and the painted witch doctors will evaporate in the dark night, I thought to myself.

'You do not mind losing your culture?' I asked.

'You mean you would have preferred me to be a caveman always?' Nicanor said.

Later, as we left, Nicanor's wife appeared briefly. Bespectacled, and hair neatly tied in a bow, she half hid behind him and smiled at us nervously. As we walked away I looked back towards the house on stilts. Nicanor remained standing on the veranda, wife and mother-in-law still beside him. The house seemed to have produced no children, but what did it matter? This triple alliance ensured the Colorados' march into civilisation as a worthy partner of the Ecuadorian state and in the future there would be no need for chiefs or even a reserve. I knew that Martín Bueno had already won his election.

'You wanna go back to my place?' Fredo asked when we had woken him from his sleep.

'No, just take us to the bus station, we're on our way to the coast,' I said.

The bus followed the oil pipeline along a road filled with pot-holes – part of the main highway from Quito to the port of Esmeraldas. We left the mountains behind us and motored through a parched landscape where the leaves no longer sighed but rustled, and where giant ants had made huge excavations in the sand. There were no clouds and at times the sky seemed to take on the yellowish mist of the earth. Inside the bus the atmosphere was stifling – a mixture of heat and dust which left us half-dazed. It was not difficult to imagine why the nomads had chosen to go much further inland to where the forest took on the colours of a thousand moths and butterflies and where the fruit was abundant and the river was a permanent source of life even in the driest season. But soon the air cleared a little and we knew that we were approaching the coast. Esmeraldas, the first port on the Pacific we came to, bore the scars of mismanagement and exploitation. Its refinery and oil terminals, its heavy commercial traffic, had poisoned the surrounding ocean so that the Pacific – the most poetic sounding of all seascapes – had been turned into a reservoir of lifeless water, where even the most aggressive wave had been transformed into a pale, insipid gel, and where fishermen – mostly descendants of the first black slaves – now spent most of their time sleeping in dug-out canoes.

It was on dry land, in the steamy back streets of this faded sea resort, that you could glimpse a life that seemed more African than South American: the large black women with their baskets of bananas, the smell of peanuts, the local *salsa* sound – a mix of calypso and rock – blaring from the café jukeboxes, the Asian traders, the collective disorder of the urchins and the whores. There were no election posters here and I doubted if there were any rulers.

At Atacamas, twenty-five kilometres down the coast, where a semblance of the Pacific has been restored, memories are stirred of the 1960s when all of us were younger. It is the resting place for local luminaries, anarchists and all those who have 'done' the Latin American trail. Just as Istanbul once provided yoghurts and hot baths on the return trip from Nepal, so Atacamas provides sun and sea for all those who are overladen with ponchos and the mysteries of the Andes. There are some Ecuadorians with intense faces, reading books on liberation theology. There are Frenchmen and Germans with paler faces, Englishmen and Americans looking like dissident boy scouts. Others wear wide-brimmed hats and are draped in ponchos and pace the beach like extras for a spaghetti Western. You cannot in truth call them hippies any more. These are the 1980s travellers. They look too well fed, too well dressed. This kind of fancy dress costs money – and though they may have smoked marihuana joints and kept tales of Borges under their pillows, they have bought return tickets before setting out on their journey and the cocaine is snorted through crisp twenty-dollar bills.

Luis is a sociology student from Quito. At night he talks of impending revolution sweeping the continent, the position of the stars, and the confluence of the ancient Indian deities. During the day he does the lotus position as he faces the sun and meditates on his nation's future. But he has become a caricature of himself, this left-over Maharishi, with his scraggy bits of hair pasted loosely on either side of his bald dome and his towel tied up around his flabby nakedness like a nappy. This disciple is immersed in prayer and meditation, but the local population regard Luis as part of the landscape along with the black ice-cream vendors jingling their bells like town criers, mermaids reclining on the crest of a wave, and Tomás, alias 'banana-skin' – a local dealer – who pontificates about the certainties of nature, keeping fit, fruit juice, and getting stoned as the easiest access to a German girl's thighs.

'Banana-skin' is tall and spindly and wears a rasta hair style. 'Now Mister Bones, don't you go looking for it. It will come to you when you least expect it. You'll wake up in the morning and there it will be, waiting for you. You won't find it but – rest assured – it will find you,' he tells me on the first day. Whether 'it' is dope or something else is not clear.

Kidge and I stayed on a deserted part of the beach in a bamboo hut belonging to the family of Antonio Febres. 'You know, I am a distant cousin of the President-to-be,' said Antonio. He was a *mestizo*, small and broad-shouldered with a permanent ring of sweat around his waist. 'Married or just lovers?' Antonio asked of us. Behind him, María was washing clothes in a stone tub with the look of someone who had emerged from a lengthy beating. We told him we were lovers in marriage. 'Love in marriage, very difficult, very difficult. Look at María, she used to be such a beautiful girl. We couldn't stop. Now she just washes clothes, cleans the pigs, it's years since we even touched each other. How long you married?'

We were sitting, the three of us, beneath a palm tree watching the Pacific turn turquoise beneath an approaching storm cloud. The trees' leaves, which had been yellow in the sunshine, were now a pinkish green and swayed in the growing wind. Near the shore, a group of pelicans flew close to the swell, their exaggerated beaks sniffing the water and their wings undulating ponderously.

'We have been married six years,' said Kidge.

Antonio looked at us, slapped a sand flea on his arm, bowed his head and sighed. 'That is a long time without children, a long time.'

Then the rain came, covering the ocean in a thick grey mist and whipping the palm trees into a frenzy. Antonio ran for cover. We were instantly drenched, the drops of water so heavy on our eyes that the whole landscape became soft and blurred at the edges. We ran into the ocean where the water was warm and thick and smelt of seaweed. Afterwards, we lay in the hut, waiting for the storm to pass, lapping and rubbing each other in dampness and in heat.

New Year's Eve. The beach, of soft whitish sand, spread out before us, pristine and deserted. The sun slid over the ocean, casting out reflections of golds and reds before dipping behind the hills of the hinterland. Just before darkness fell, Charles appeared in the distance like a shipwrecked sailor washed ashore. He was paddling through the shallow water, nimbly and distractedly with his trousers rolled up and a peaked cap resting awkwardly on the side of his head.

'I thought you'd end up here,' he said with a huge smile when he had reached us. 'You see there's nowhere to go after Atacamas. It's the end of the road.'

Just before midnight we joined a group of Ecuadorians near the shore. They had gathered a pile of broken palms and placed on top of them an effigy of a *conquistador*. They were holding candles and whispering to each other. One of them, a large woman with a billowing skirt, stepped forward towards the pile and began to read out a proclamation in a loud, theatrical voice. 'Hear ye, hear ye,' she said in old Spanish, holding the document to the light of the moon. She then broke into plainchant so that her words echoed across the beach like a litany.

'Don Gonzalo, you are tonight condemned to take your final bow, to sit on your final throne, to be castrated, and pulled limb from limb, to be finally speared a thousand times and burnt at the stake. We who are gathered here bear witness to the banishment of evil and the ushering in of all that is good and plenty. TO THE DEVIL, DON GONZALO, AND MAY WE NEVER SEE YOU AGAIN.'

And with that, Don Gonzalo was engulfed in flames and for an instant his tormented body cast a struggling shadow across the water. Then he vanished like a genie, and the Old Year went out, in an explosion of fireworks, and the old woman, who had appeared from nowhere, danced around the smouldering stake, beating the embers with a stick. 'To the Devil, Don Gonzalo, to the Devil,' everyone chanted in unison. Then the woman turned and walked around the circle, kissing each person on the lips.

'What a wonderful moment,' said Charles, 'I haven't been embraced like that by anyone in my life.'

It was the first dance of a New Year and as I watched the demons expurgated around the campfire I resolved that the next twelve months would be better than the last. At sunrise, we jumped on the back of Charles's truck and began retracing our steps, before leaving Ecuador for Peru.

— 7 —

UNDER THE SUN

To arrive at Lima airport is to realise instantly that Peru is a nation that cares little about how others perceive it. In other cities governments accept that the airport and its immediate environment are a nation's first statement. In South America, in particular, it is the status symbol, the image on which a regime and a system stand to be judged. It is at the airport, not at ports and mountain borders, that foreign dignitaries and businessmen arrive, where attitudes matter. In Buenos Aires, the junta had buried the 'disappeared' in the forest near the international airport before sowing the area with grass. They then built a motorway all the way to the centre of town. But in Lima no one had bothered.

Beyond passport control men with shifty faces waited, offering taxis in the manner of those who offer whores. There were policemen fingering sub-machine-guns. There seemed to be a high risk of being caught in a cataclysmic crossfire, and arriving passengers instinctively clustered in groups.

'Want to share a taxi to town? It'll be more reliable,' one tourist said.

'Do you know of a good hotel?' asked another.

'This airport gives me the creeps,' said a third.

Beyond the airport was a shanty town. Others I had seen in South America had a temporary, transient look about them. You felt that the sheet iron and makeshift latrines could be taken down just as easily as they had been put up. But this one seemed to have been around for many years. It rarely rains in Lima, so the squat, square blocks of sandy earth used as homes had been moulded into the dust and had given the periphery the aspect of a desert town.

'What happens when it rains?' I asked.

'Oh, it's very rare,' said Pedro, 'but if it rains, the huts melt like candles.' Pedro weighed at least sixteen stone, must have been in his mid-fifties, and had the dark yellowish features of his Indian ancestors.

He was the only person I had remotely trusted at the airport. Whereas everyone else had shouted and hassled, he had gone on sitting on a crate of Coca-Cola. He was reading a newspaper and smoking a hand-rolled cigarette and seemed oblivious to the time of day or the nature of the airport's latest arrivals.

When we first approached him, he had asked us to leave him alone as he was having his afternoon break. 'But you won't have trouble getting a lift from one of those sharks,' he had said before burying himself in the sports page. We pestered him, begging deliverance from the sea of sharks, and he agreed under certain conditions.

'If you come with Pedro, you have to accept that it's Bartolomé taking us and that Bartolomé likes taking his time. He is reliable and good and my best friend but he's not a shark, he's a tortoise.' I looked around for his companion. I imagined an old man, perhaps a cripple. But there was no one, not even a dog hiding behind the crate. Pedro noted our perplexity and with a huge grin slapped the bonnet of his taxi.

'Bartolomé saved us from extinction and he still does today.'

The vehicle had been named after Father Bartolomé de las Casas, a Dominican friar who in the sixteenth century devoted a lifetime to the work of securing fair treatment for the Indians after the Spanish conquest. Las Casas had conducted a major public debate before the Imperial Court, arguing that the Indians, being subjects of the Spanish Crown, should enjoy equal rights with the Spaniards and that the colonists should support themselves by their own efforts and that they had no right to enforced labour.

Las Casas aroused intense opposition from those with a vested interest in the supply of native labour and from theologians as con-vinced of the righteousness of their cause. The chief of these was Juan Ginés de Sepúlveda, who argued that the Aristotelian doctrine of natural slavery was entirely applicable to the Indians on the grounds of their 'natural inferiority'. The debate proved inconclusive. As the centuries passed, the Indians' descendants were allowed only a token advance on the social scale – from slaves to second-class citizens.

Pedro took us very slowly towards the city. The air smelt of diesel mixed with urine. It was heavily polluted and seemed to have had all moisture sucked from it. There was a hectic, chaotic movement of people. They clung to overcrowded buses, jumped traffic lights, col-lided with each other on the broken pavements. The dust swirled and framed the situation in a yellowish haze. The crowds were made up of half-castes and Indians, scarcely a white among them.

We left the mud huts behind, manoeuvring our way through streets where past and present co-existed in an architectural free-for-all. There was no immediately clear definition here as in Quito, but a more disordered grafting of graceless modern blocks on to the ribs of decayed palaces. Pedro left us at a hotel that seemed to have been expropriated in some distant revolution. It had been one of the city's luxury additions once, complete with phones, televisions and room service. But none of its services functioned any more. Instead an ageing bell porter accompanied us to a room no one had bothered to clean, where the sheets used by the previous occupant lay crumpled on the edge of a bed.

The tourist map suggested a walk through the shopping streets of Lima to the Plaza de Armas, where the city had managed to retain a semblance of architectural purpose. Here were to be found the remnants of the City of the Kings founded by the *conquistador* Francisco Pizarro in 1535 in all its imperial and post-colonial splendour – cathedral, government palace, and Archbishop's residence gathered round a seventeenth-century bronze fountain.

The Spaniards had marked out Lima in straight lines and forty-five degree angles, and yet the chaos I had witnessed on the outskirts became more concentrated the nearer we came to the centre. The people had abandoned geometry; they surged this way and that, ran, crowded into shops. There was a scarcely hidden aggression in the antics of the street vendors. As you passed, they thrust everything at you from a mangled puppy to a piece of reproduction Inca silver. A clown played a record on an old gramophone and then smashed it against the nearest pillar. An urchin kicked another urchin in the mouth. Near them a dwarf without arms or legs spun his trunk on a wooden board, and uttered a demented squeal. The atmosphere of simmering violence was reflected in the newspaper headlines: 'BARRACKS ATTACKED', 'CHILD HELD FOR RANSOM', 'DELINQUENT ATTACKS BANK', 'CHILDREN BURNT TO DEATH', they declared. Each story was as grizzly as the next. Peruvians seemed to have nothing else to read about except football.

In the Plaza de Armas there were many more policemen than civilians. A smallish crowd of tourists had gathered outside the presidential palace to watch the guard in their white uniforms and plumes as they slow-marched across a courtyard. Japanese clicked obsessively with their cameras unaware that an eerie silence seemed to have descended over the city. At each entrance to the Plaza, detachments of riot police stood in awkward formation. Short muskets tipped with gas canisters protruded from their grey uniforms. Then an officer with a whip walked over to us and told us to leave the Plaza.

'We are tourists,' I said.

'Well, tourism is cancelled today,' the officer said. Across the square, two police trucks with water cannon had taken up positions near the bronze statue as if to underline the point. We decided it was best to leave.

As we walked back to the hotel, we passed groups of students setting fire to parts of the city – a car here, a newspaper stand there. Sometimes they lobbed their Molotov cocktails at nothing in particular and left them simmering on the empty pavement. There were some students who shouted slogans for university reform and cheaper bus fares as they waved red flags or hid behind handkerchiefs. Others seemed simply to chase their own shadows along the wall, like effete ballet dancers. On one street corner they had captured a policeman and were subjecting him to an impromptu 'people's trial'. This consisted in having him pose dejected and humiliated between two student 'guards' as a group of photographers snapped the scene for posterity. Then the gas filtered through the streets and the shots rang out beyond the Plaza and we ran the rest of the way to the hotel.

Through most of the night there was the sound of distant detonations and occasional gunfire, and then around three o'clock in the morning someone blew up an electricity pylon and our hotel and most of the surrounding area was plunged into darkness. 'It's the Shining Path,' someone whispered in the corridor.

It was in 1980 that Shining Path had first announced its existence by hanging dogs from telephone wires in Lima and burning ballot boxes in the southern town of Ayacucho. The organisation's founder was Abimael Guzmán, a philosophy student and dissident of the Peruvian Communist Party who, with messianic zeal, pursued his vision of a 'fourth sword of Marxism', in the wake of Marx, Lenin and Mao. Guzmán claimed Marxism–Leninism had lost its 'purity' in the 're-visionism' of Moscow and Peking and that there was a need to eradicate old structures and set up a popular republic. Guzmán's 'Shining Path' organisation took its name from the political theories of José Carlos Mariátegui, another Peruvian Marxist, who had predicted that pure Marxism–Leninism would open the 'shining path to revolution'.

From its earliest action, Sendero Luminoso had spread its field of operations gradually, recruiting among the peasants in the south of Peru through a mixture of ideological persuasion and terrorism. By the time we arrived in Peru Sendero guerrillas had earned a reputation as South America's Khmer Rouge – fanatical, cruel and ruthless in their killings and torture of political opponents. In the south their influence was taken so seriously that thirteen provinces were under military control.

The morning after the explosion, we met Pedro again. I asked him what he thought about Sendero Luminoso.

'It's the biggest problem we have here. They are pushing this country into chaos and the government doesn't know what to do with them. In South America we have always been used to guerrillas that are here one day and gone the next – a bit of revolution then a military coup and it's all over. But Sendero is different. It goes on and on, and no one wins, so the country is in a permanent state of unresolved violence,' Pedro said.

'Have they the support of the people?' I asked.

'Perhaps, but you have to understand there is a lot of fear, many people disappear, no one knows what happens to them or who's responsible. Some say it's Sendero, but others say it's the army. It's a war without rules.'

'Disappeared.' It was a word that before coming to South America I had identified with fairy tales. Subsequently it came to be redefined as part of a gruesome lie. It was a category the Argentine military had first invented to excuse the kidnapping, torture and murder of thousands of political opponents. To say someone had died was to admit responsibility, but to describe someone as 'disappeared' was to cast doubt over existence itself. To the relatives of the victims it was the cruellest of methods, where nothing was certain, not even the manner of death.

'I know what you're thinking,' Pedro said. His cigarette was even bigger than the one I had seen him light that first time at the airport. It rested on the dashboard, smouldering. 'You think this is something peculiar to this crazy age we live in, the age of failed democracies and sophisticated military coups. But you forget history goes back further than yesterday.'

And so it was that on the morning after the student riots Pedro drove us to the place where the Court of the Inquisition had presided in the seventeenth century. There, a woman in white socks and a neat blue suit sold us a ticket. I marvelled at the ceiling. It was intricately carved in mahogany.

'The torture chamber is down those steps to the left,' the woman said. Her tone was clipped, not so much bossy as irritable. Boredom had long since undermined the challenge of authority.

I went on looking at the ceiling.

'The torture chamber . . . ' she began again. She offered us a guidebook in English. 'It tells you all you need to know. All the artefacts and protagonists are carefully listed and there are photographs . . . ' she said, brushing imaginary specks of dust from her ticket box.

'I'm Spanish,' I said, 'like the Holy Inquisition.' Pedro then nudged me from behind and we walked on down the steps.

In the basement there was a smell of chewing gum and wax. The excited cackle of a group of Peruvian schoolgirls reverberated around the stone walls. A Japanese in a short-sleeved white shirt pushed and shoved his way through, before photographing a tableau of a model heretic being garrotted. The names of the one hundred Indians who had been stretched, broken and finally burnt for not confessing to the faith had been inscribed in gold on wooden plaques. Lest we forget . . .

'Heroes or victims?' I asked Pedro.

'Both, perhaps. We open this to the public as if to say: "Look, this is what Peru used to be under the terrible Spanish rule. This is the Peru we overcame." We can only show a museum and not the reality because we are civilised today. But we all know that more people have been killed by Sendero and the military than by the Inquisition.'

'So why did you bring us here?'

'To show you what we are and what we are not,' said Pedro. He had taken out a penknife and was scraping a plaque where one of the schoolgirls had stuck her gum.

We crossed one of the few remaining historical landmarks of the city – the seventeenth-century Roman-style bridge with grey slabs of stone legend insisted had been bound together with thousands of egg whites. Earthquakes through the ages had shaken Lima to its foundations, but the bridge over the River Rimac had remained constant in the midst of an ever-changing landscape of crumbling houses and emerging tower blocks. On one side of the bridge were the impeccable presidential guard, performing their daily goose-step ritual as if yesterday's riot had never happened. On the other, gathered down secret rubbish-filled alleyways, were the washerwomen, bent double over stone fonts, whispering as they wrung away the city's dirt. Their hands were as rough as reptile skin and they had thick, strong arms. One woman was probably no more than thirty but she looked much older. Quite soon into our conversation, she showed us her foot, smudged with varicose veins and a poorly healed gash. 'Once I was working out in the field with the children and I stepped on a piece of split cane. A splinter went through my foot as easily as a sharp knife cuts through a cooked potato. The nearest village was two miles away, so I walked for two miles. There were no doctors, but they took the splinter out and gave me salt. Washing, you see, keeps you out of harm's way,' she said. As she went on scrubbing, the water splashed on to the dusty ground, causing foam-tipped rivulets of muddy water to slide back down the alleyway to where the River Rimac moved like an insidious snake.

We walked on to the church of Santo Domingo, where I had heard poor Peruvians sought solace with one of the world's few black saints. In South America, being black is inferior even to being Indian, so since his death in 1639 San Martín de Porres, a black friar who had achieved sainthood by having no other ambition than to sweep floors with a broomstick, had engrained himself in the popular consciousness as a form of reassurance. The graffiti scribbled near the place where his bones once lay, were mostly pledges of conversion. 'Help us be good' said one. 'Please let me grow up to be a poet,' said another. There were phrases that smacked of suffering and a peculiarly Indian stoicism. For instance, 'I have lost my first six children. Help me to keep my seventh.' I would have been happy to leave the kind, selfless San Martín just with these scattered personal confessions. And yet someone had felt the necessity to write in wider, more blackened lettering than all the others, the only testimony to Peru past and present: 'Viva Sendero Luminoso.'

Miraflores, Lima's residential area, straddles, like an outer planet, the Pacific coast. A long avenue leads you away from the bustle and the smells and the squat mud houses without roofs into an atmosphere scented with flowers and spotted with colour. We passed by the American Embassy, surrounded by walls and presided over by marines with shaven heads, into suburbs littered with the remnants of more glorious times. There were houses with white towers where the plaster had cracked and formed dark tributaries; wooden lodges leaning on

stilts like the homes of some forgotten witch's tale. Across the doorways, elaborate crests of arms echoed the decadence of a nobility
overtaken by history. I had been told that in the homes once lived in
by Spanish aristocrats there were now bankers and Generals and
Russian diplomats. On the outer walls of their homes, dark splodges
of graffiti screamed defiance, resurrecting the spirits of old Inca re-
bellions and more recent aggressions. In the middle of Miraflores we
stopped near a small park surrounded by a high fence. As we walked
towards it, we were overtaken by two young urchins. They jumped
on to the fence, and clung there, gaping at the park beyond.

'Just look at those tits,' said one.

'I shit on her tits, it's the ass that counts,' said the other. The
subject of their gaze were two Indian nannies who were sitting near a
flowerbed surrounded by a group of blond children. The children
were building palaces with their bricks and eating ice-cream and their
locks glittered in the sun like wheat at harvest time. One of the nannies
giggled nervously. But her colleague spat at the ground. 'Go away or
I'll call the police,' she screamed at the urchins. These nannies were
on the other side of the fence once. But now they were surrogate
mothers to the immaculate children of the rich.

'In the whole of old Peru,' wrote the sixteenth-century *mestizo* chron-
icler Garcilaso de la Vega, 'there is undoubtedly no place as revered
as the imperial city of Cuzco, which is where all the Inca Kings hold
court and establish the seat of government.'

It was difficult to think of Cuzco on the plane that took us towards
it, away from the Pacific shoreline and along the Andean *cordillera*
which runs south-east from Lima. The passenger nearest to us was a
teacher in her mid-twenties called Ana.

'Tourism. The more of it we have the better, because without it
we're lost, really lost. I used to be a student once and did what all
students do. Read Marx and throw Molotovs, but then I woke up one
day and realised that everyone was the same – students, priests,
politicians, Generals, they were all part of the same mess that is Peru.
The only way we can save ourselves is by getting foreigners to pay for
our economic recovery.'

I asked Ana who and what she taught.

'I teach Peruvians how to speak English. It's a good imperialist
language,' she said.

Down the corridor, an air steward was announcing that the cabin staff were about to begin a game of Bingo. Our score cards, he told us, were clipped to the emergency instructions pamphlet. Soon he was picking out the numbers from a black hat and enunciating them in jingles. 'Clickety-click . . . sixty-six . . . my oh my . . . forty-nine . . .' His voice seemed strangely disembodied like that of a ventriloquist.

The plane was hit by turbulence and out of the window I could see the sides of the mountains, looming like monsters from a stormy sea.

Ana gripped her seat. 'Do you think we are going to crash?'

I began to tell her not to worry as Peruvian pilots were used to this sort of weather. Then the cabin staff, as suddenly as they had started, stopped the Bingo game. There was a collective gasp and a single voice that rose above the others protesting that he only had one number left to complete the card.

This is the way the world ends, I thought, not with a bang, but with a whimper of bingo players – no final words, just numbers. Ana was now perspiring heavily and reciting the Hail Mary. But she worried unnecessarily. Within minutes the plane jerked once more, lurched sharply to one side, righted itself and descended rapidly between the mountain tops, through the valley that leads to the Imperial City.

'When two Indians meet on a road leading to the city, the one who is going there immediately greets the one coming from there as his superior . . . ' wrote Garcilaso de la Vega.

No one was greeting anybody at Cuzco airport that morning when finally we landed. Because of an earlier storm, outgoing and incoming flights had been delayed, so we were confronted by groups of tired-looking tourists. The first Indian I saw was being shouted at by an American in a panama hat.

'Do you realise what you've done? You've gonna got the wrong suitcase and left mine back at the hotel. Now I'm going to miss my damn plane because of you.'

The Indian bowed his head, and shook it from side to side. 'Me no work hotel, me work airport, very sorry,' he said. He was holding the two mistaken suitcases and shaking with the strain of their weight.

'You're saying you don't work at the hotel and it's not your fault? Well I'll tell ya somethin. Bullshit,' said the man in the panama hat. He was about to take a swipe at the Indian, but changed his mind and walked off.

Once the American had left, the Indian dropped the suitcase to the ground. As it fell, it opened and spilled its contents of books and clothes on to the pavement. The Indian spat on them and walked away.

Cuzco at a distance seemed a city that was perfectly contained and unified. The town was neatly defined with its lines of tiled roofs and stone walls and whitewash as if a part of Castilian Spain had been transported and set here in Cuzco – the 'navel of the earth'. On glimpsing it for the first time, Pizarro had also been reminded of his own country, but he was to write later that Cuzco was of such fine quality as 'would be remarkable even in Spain'. The nearer we walked to the city centre, the more impressive the town became. The houses had massive wooden doors and ornately carved balconies and stood on the foundation stones earlier laid by the Incas. The thick blocks lay fitted tightly together in complex polygonal patterns, their joints so precise they seemed moulded together with putty. Through the centuries, other buildings in Cuzco had collapsed during earthquakes, other walls had cracked beneath the rain and the sun, but these thick stones had survived as a lasting testimony to the Incas' skill as masons. However narrow the street, however poor the quarter, these stones had endured.

The early history of Cuzco has been confused by legend. It was the young Garcilaso de la Vega, at the age of sixteen, who had first expressed his bafflement when confronted with so much uncertainty. Going up to one of the Inca elders, he had said, 'The Spanish and the nations that are their neighbours possess books, they know their entire history, and can even say how many thousands of years ago God created heaven and earth. But you have none, how are you able to tell us of your past?'

Mythology sustained the Inca in his early conquests and domination of local tribes. According to oral tradition it was the demigod Manco Cápac who emerged from a cave called Tambo-toco at Pararitacambo, near to the present site of Cuzco, before founding the Imperial City in the fertile valley with a golden hand plough sometime between the eleventh and twelfth centuries.

Manco Cápac's great-grandchildren were born with a full set of teeth. At the age of one they were as big as an average eight year old, and at two they were already fit for battle. But it was Parachuti, a later descendant, who is credited with the civic planning of Cuzco and the erection of many of its most important buildings in the early fourteenth century, such as the Temples of the Sun, Moon, and Stars, and the Palace of the Serpents, the architectural remains of which are

visible today. The expansion of the Inca Empire – which the imperial
city of Cuzco reflected – was certainly dramatic. In a period of little
more than fifty years, Parachuti and his son Topa Inca extended their
domination for almost three thousand miles along the Andes, from
central Chile to what is today Colombia. Cuzco became the spiritual
and administrative centre of the Empire, South America's equivalent
of Byzantium. Within the city were built the residences of the Inca
Kings, their pantheons, courts and holy images.

And yet the Empire, for all its myths and glories, was based on
totalitarian deviousness. The Incas claimed solar descent for their
royal families. Manco Cápac used a suit of shining armour to reflect
the sun's rays and deceive the people. Subsequently a golden disc was
placed in the Temple of the Sun for the same end. When the Spaniards
came, they melted down the gold and shattered the illusion.

As we roamed through Cuzco, I reflected on the ornaments and
palaces, the fine food and clothing, and the grandiose rituals that had
once been a part of life, and contrasted them with the Inca descendants
who now shuffled here, crouched there, begged and murmured, resigned to the latest foreign invasion. In the Plaza de Armas, the Incas
had once conducted their most elaborate of ceremonies. But the square
we saw was deserted except for an Indian woman standing upright
next to a black llama. Her plaited black hair fell on to her shoulders
from beneath a brown woollen hat and a pair of sandalled feet stood
flat-footed under a fading pink skirt.

'You want a photograph, you pay ten dollars,' she said pushing the
llama in front of me. I settled for two dollars and snapped her picture.
Then it began to rain and we ran into the cathedral for cover. The
building had been built in the seventeenth century on the site of a
ruined Inca palace. Its exaggerated style reflected the extent to which
the Spaniards had aped the grandeur of the vanquished. The high altar
was solid silver backed with carved mahogany. The sacristy was filled
with priceless chalices and gold-encrusted vestments. In a dimly lit
chapel, a group of old Indian women were chanting monotonously in
Quechua, the Incas' language, to the accompaniment of a violin played
by an old man in a black poncho. Before the group, a broken Christ-
on-the-cross figure had turned black from the heat of so much candle
flame. In the half-light, the women and the violinist melted in each
other's shadows, while their chanting rose to a wail and echoed
through the cathedral.

On our way out, we passed two works of art which seemed to

encapsulate the cultural tension which had survived in Cuzco. The first was a painting dating from the late colonial period. It depicted a scene from the Last Supper with eleven white apostles and an Indian Judas. The other was the wooden choir loft. Much of it was carved with angels and saints rising towards heaven, but in the confusion of images a lone Indian artisan had managed to slip in a serpent and a piece of corn as a lasting witness to the world of spirits and superstition shared by the common people. It was a reminder that whereas the official Inca religion, with its deceptions, had quickly been supplanted by Christianity, a more basic idolatry of sorcerers and talismans had survived.

It was no longer raining when we left the cathedral, but the town seemed to be awash with running streams. The brownish water cascaded down the steps and along the narrow streets, oozed from between the narrow crevices of the grey stone blocks, dripped like oil from the doors and niches. Where the Indian woman and the llama had been, another woman was washing some clothes in a huge puddle. Near her stood a pair of soldiers clutching sub-machine-guns under plastic capes. One of them took his gun out and poked the clothes that were piled beside the woman, while the other questioned her in Quechua. When they had finished with her, she gathered her clothes and, nodding her head, walked into the cathedral. Next, across the square came a group of tourists led by a guide who held an umbrella up to the sky like a standard. The tourists were all dressed in identical black raincoats and walked behind their guide in tight formation as if they had been militarised. I asked one of the soldiers if tourists in Cuzco always marched rather than walked.

'It's safer that way,' the soldier answered curtly.

Soon the square was ringed with pairs of soldiers as it filled with tourists and Indians with llamas, and the main crowd converged on the church of La Compañía de Jesús to celebrate the Day of the Epiphany. Garcilaso de la Vega had written:

Such a vast number of people assembled every day that they could only crowd into the square with great difficulty. Manco had all the dead ancestors brought to the festivities. After he had gone with a great entourage to the temple to make an oration to the sun, throughout the morning he proceeded in rotation to the tombs where each dead Inca was embalmed. They were then removed with great veneration and reverence, and brought into the city seated on their thrones in order of precedence. There was a litter for each one, with men in its livery to carry it. The natives came down in this way, singing many ballads and giving thanks to the sun.

Down from the mountain came the Three Kings. Their images stood effetely atop a small platform in the shape of small dolls dressed in crimson silk and broad hats. They were carried on the shoulders of Indians in their shirtsleeves. The carriers swayed at odd angles, as if drunk, laughed and cursed and tripped over their own feet, while behind them a brass band played a military march and small boys let off fireworks.

We followed the procession into the old, dark Jesuit church, where the Palace of the Serpents had once been. It was already filled with Indian women. Many of them had part of their huge skirts draped over the bench in front of them; there were also many children eating whatever their mothers produced from their pockets. On entering the church the band had fallen silent. But now it started up again in a quick military march so that the church was soon filled with the sound of battles and the smell of alcohol. 'They're all drunk,' said an old woman with long grey hair, as she crunched up a banana peel and threw it on to the floor.

There were so many people, and both men and women were such heavy drinkers, and they poured so much into their skins – for their entire activity was drinking, not eating – that it is a fact that two wide drains over half a foot in diameter which emptied into the river beneath the flagstones . . . ran with urine throughout the day from those who urinated into them, as abundantly as a flowing spring. This was not remarkable when one considers the amount they were drinking and the numbers drinking. But the sight was a marvel and something never seen before.

That night in the hotel, a local tourist guide told us about eight Peruvian journalists who had been found in a remote mountain village near to Cuzco hacked to pieces after setting off to investigate the latest Sendero offensive. It was a story I had already read about in the Argentine newspapers but which recounted locally seemed all the more disquieting. The official government explanation of their deaths was that they had been murdered by terrorists. But the official version had overlooked or simply chosen to ignore the evidence provided by a number of key witnesses who insisted that the journalists had been butchered by peasants acting under military orders.

The guide was anxious to talk, but there was something in the way he volunteered his information that made me mistrust him. So I abandoned the conversation and we went for a pre-bed stroll through the town. Cuzco was bathed in moonlight and a cold breeze swept through the streets. They were empty except for the odd military patrol here and there and the occasional tourist. Once I heard a single gun shot far off followed by the sound of dogs barking, but then the streets were hung in silence again. Walking through the squares of Cuzco and its Inca ruins, the memory of the murdered journalists seemed to touch the city with a deep-rooted sadness. For these buildings had witnessed far worse butcheries in the course of the centuries. They had begun with the sacrifices to the sun, continued with the torture and executions of the defeated Incas, and found their contemporary expression in the unresolved power struggle between Sendero and the military. The murder of the journalists might have shocked the outside world, but in Peru it was interpreted as something akin to a ritual. The methods used against them were no more brutal than those the Spaniards had used against Túpac Amaru. In 1781, near to the place where we were walking that night, the direct descendant of the Inca Emperors had had his tongue cut off and his arms and legs pulled from his body by four horses, before being finally beheaded. Then his severed limbs were carved into several bits and distributed among the neighbouring villages, and his torso was burnt and thrown into the River Watanay.

The next day we caught the train to Machu Picchu. Engine '485', snub-nosed and painted bright orange with red stripes, pulled us in a broad arc above Cuzco. As the train hissed and grated its way up into the hills, small children emerged from crude huts covered in rough thatch. They rubbed the dirt into their faces, and ruffled their hair. One of them yawned while urinating against the side of the hut. Another picked up some stones and threw them at the train. Behind them a group of suckling pigs shuffled forward before digging their snouts into a pile of loose garbage. Most of the huts had clothes hanging from them, but one or two had dried bits of llama meat and strange talismans.

My fellow passengers were talking to each other about the photographs they'd taken the day before, about the relative merits of this hotel and that, where to buy the best ponchos in Ecuador, or blankets in Peru, and how the thinness of the Andean air made them feel sick.

Soon '485' was picking up speed along the great plain of Anta, the setting for the epic fifteenth-century battle between the Incas and the neighbouring Chanca tribe, the outcome of which launched the former on a course of ruthless imperialist expansion. Across the marshy lands, wild horses broke into flight at the noise of the train and hunch-backed cows huddled together nervously. Here and there groups of peasants carrying bundles of corn followed the railway line. Miracu-lously some of them seemed to have caught up with us when our train suddenly stopped a few miles further along. They were waiting with their corn cobs freshly grilled over open fires. We ate one each and shared a bottle of *chicha* with one of the railway staff. He said the drink was the purest on earth as it had been made from maize and fermented thanks to the saliva of his girlfriend. It tasted like stale cider and had the same lulling effect on both Kidge and me.

The Indian who had sold us our meal, moved down the train with his remaining corn laid out in a broad basket covered with a yellowish piece of cloth.

'Take those away, I don't want to be poisoned,' said a Chilean tourist. The Indian moved on silently.

'The Indians say this is the sacred corn. If someone were to die from it, the world would end,' said her husband.

'Nonsense,' the woman said. And then she bought herself a bar of Cadbury's chocolate from the train's bar.

North of Anta, the hills were greener and were sprinkled with tufts of wild yellow flowers. The train filled with the scent of herbs. The hills were lined with the jagged stones of the Inca terraces. Although some of them had been restored, there seemed to be little agricultural activity on the steep slopes. Instead the occasional peasant used the linked passageways and drainage channels as a safe pathway between villages. It was along here too that the great American explorer Hiram Bingham had trekked in 1909 after setting out from Cuzco on his journey of discovery to Machu Picchu. As we left the barren landscape behind us and penetrated the tropical vegetation that clings to the middle reaches of the Andes, I began to share his wonder at the sheer beauty of the region. The rapids of the Urubamba river twisted their way through the canyon, teasingly tossing stones up in the air and spraying the windows of the train. '485' screeched like a demented bird and its sound echoed through the mountains. These rose sheer into the sky, their gigantic precipices encrusted with rocks or streaked with cascades, piled upon one another just as Bingham had seen them.

'It was the majestic grandeur of the Canadian Rockies, as well as the startling beauty of the Nuuanu Pali near Honolulu, and the enchanting vistas of the Koolau Ditch on Maui. In the variety of its charms and the power of its spell, I know of no place in the world which can compare with it.'

'485' stopped where the ground levelled and the river widened and where the undergrowth had crept down from the mountainside and encroached upon the railway line. So great was the sound of rushing water that to step off the train was to feel yourself placed momentarily beneath a waterfall. By now the day was fading and the vegetation was dripping with humidity. A thin mist had begun to shroud the mountains. A bus took us the rest of the way to the heights of Machu Picchu, winding its way towards the higher peaks. For the first time since leaving Cuzco, the tourists had fallen silent, half awestruck, half terrified by the sheer drop on either side of the road and the mass of vegetation that spread out across the valley, which was covered in wild orchids and lupins. When we reached the top the silence broke, as the tourists tumbled out and raced towards the ruins. By then we had decided to wait until the bus had taken them down the hill again so we could see Machu Picchu by ourselves.

The next day we watched the dawn break over Machu Picchu. The sun's rays moved slowly across the gigantic mountains of granite. Against a black backdrop, first one peak then another became illuminated, the upper reaches cut off from the rest by a collar of pinkish mist. Like a piece of creation, Machu Picchu was revealed to us in slow motion, the light spreading as it fell down towards the ruins. Now the breadth and scope of each mountain was defined as the mist evaporated, leaving only thin wisps, and the sun grew bolder. Each mountain seemed to resemble a giant animal rising from sleep. Under the sun, in the morning brightness, Huayna Picchu, which overlooks the site, was a gargantuan silver-lined lion crouching and ready to pounce. We walked slowly round the ruined city. A lone llama sat on the edge of the mountainside regurgitating grass, a mongrel sprang from nowhere and snapped at our feet before disappearing. We walked along the terraces, and through the perfectly constructed arches and temples. As in Cuzco, you could not but marvel at the way the stones were held tightly against each other without cement. And the sheer position of the city, set high up in a mountain enclave like something that has fallen to earth from another planet, made the scene doubly impressive. We felt very small in the midst of a creation of such scope and scale.

There has been much debate about the origins of Machu Picchu. Bingham wrote that this was the legendary lost city of the Andes which pre-dated the Incas and which in its last state became the 'carefully guarded treasure house where that precious worship of the sun, the moon, the thunder and the stars, so violently overthrown in Cuzco, was restored'. A more recent theory suggests that South America's most famous ruin was just one more royal residence and 'pleasure house' amongst those that dotted the Inca Empire. And yet even today it is a mystery that has yet to be fully unravelled, and it is doubtful that it ever will be with any certainty.

— 8 —

BEYOND THE PRAIRIES

Far away and long ago, the great expanse of Argentine prairie known as the *pampa* was an image of South American prosperity. One of the world's oldest land masses, it stretches from the foothills of the Andes in the west to the Atlantic Ocean in the east. To the north it is bordered by the semi-tropical banks of the River Paraná, and to the south by the River Colorado, which marks the beginning of Patagonia. From earliest times, erosion by the elements has forged hundreds of feet of sediment, fine clay, sand and dust, to create a vast temperate and fertile zone, covering 650,000 square kilometres.

In the first half of the twentieth century, the region had a *per capita* income higher than Sweden or Switzerland, a foreign trade larger than Canada's. It was one of the main exporters of cereals and meat products and was known as the 'granary of the world'. Now the region is but a mirror of Argentina's failure as a nation, and the wasted potential of a continent. Overshadowed by the unwieldy metropolis of Buenos Aires it can barely cushion a foreign debt of over fifty billion dollars in a world unable to sustain agricultural surplus.

Julia, our first daughter, was with us on our journey across the *pampa*. Aged ten months, she sat on the back seat of the car with her mother, surrounded by nappies, bottles and tins of baby food, gurgling or half asleep, and seemingly oblivious to the many miles of hard travel that lay ahead of us.

In order to avoid the traffic and the heat, we had set off from our home in the suburb of La Lucila just before midnight. Our middle-class neighbourhood on that Saturday night was filled with young people crowding into ice-cream parlours or discos, or driving round on motorbikes. But once we had cleared the outskirts, the traffic thinned to a trickle. It was there that we stopped. Now the sky was filled with shooting stars and an ivory moon that guided our voyage as if through a tunnel. The dawn came in a reddish glow shrouded in thin

mist and flocks of white birds rising into the sky in celebration. Across
the plains, herds of cows were grazing, and small lagoons reflected
the first light in shades of oil. There was not a human in sight.
As the sun rose, all around us we saw the flat land, as glimpsed
by W. H. Hudson, 'its horizon a perfect ring of misty blue colour
where the crystal-blue dome of the sky rests on the level green
world'.

That morning, there were occasions when a car would appear as if
from nowhere and overtake us. Its occupants sat upright, staring
straight ahead. They seemed oblivious to the landscape about
them. It was as though all that mattered to them was the point of
departure, almost certainly Buenos Aires, and the point of arrival,
probably a seaside apartment or a country estate. The horizon
beckoned them, appealed to their self-interest, but they drove as if
hypnotised through a *pampa* that for them evoked neither nostalgia
nor romance.

About 150 miles south of Buenos Aires, we drove slowly into
Pirovano. Like other *pampa* towns, this one seemed to have been
diminished by the surrounding landscape. With its dull constructions
of squat rectangular houses and straight, dust-covered streets, it had
become a barren oasis in a fertile desert. Those who lived here had
settled to work the land not to enjoy each other's company. And now
that the land was no longer needed Pirovano was filled with little else
but memories.

The three of us settled for the night in the house of Leopoldo and
María, the parents of a friend in Buenos Aires. Leopoldo was second-
generation Italian, a giant of a man with a thick jaw who worked as
a temporary farm manager on one of the near-by estates. His wife
was of Spanish stock, a frail asthmatic woman with strained features
who shuffled about the house saying little and gasping for breath. On
our arrival, Leopoldo hugged me as if encountering a long-lost friend
and wasted little time before toasting our good health with a succession
of wine bottles. Gathered in a small, damp kitchen, we were joined
by Leopoldo's father, Carlo, a diminutive old man who nodded his
head and mumbled incomprehensibly to himself.

As María fed us on fish pie and cakes, Leopoldo launched his attack
on the state of Argentina, raising his voice in an ever-rising circle of
impassioned outbursts. The country had lost a war . . . the country
was bankrupt . . . the country had had its worst floods in fifty years
. . . the government had changed the currency for the third time in

ten years and it was still not worth the paper it was printed on . . . it was a nation of pirates and con-men and corrupt Generals who didn't know how to fight . . .

Leopoldo's voice trembled, his eyes grew tearful . . . : 'Fish, do you see this? . . . fish that's what we've come round to, vegetarians in the middle of the *pampa*. Why, you may ask, when there is so much cattle do we have to eat fish? Because the government says that we've hit the low point of the beef cycle and we haven't enough meat for domestic consumption. Can you believe it? And we were once a people that believed that God was an Argentine.'

Then Leopoldo had a coughing fit. His face grew large and red and his saliva spluttered over the table. When it was over, he staggered to his feet like a man shot in the chest, and walked from the room without saying a word. He left behind a terrible silence.

The next morning, on my way to breakfast, I came across Carlo in a covered patio at the back of the house. His face was set in a childlike smile as it appeared from behind some geraniums. He was barefoot and dressed in a pale blue nightgown and was holding a large piece of flint. 'I thought I'd get the equipment ready for the day,' he said pointing to a hand plough in the corner. On the *pampa* ploughs like this hadn't been used for at least thirty years; they pre-dated the combine harvester and the tractor. But Carlo set about it with his flint as if its use was eternal. As he worked into the rust, Carlo volunteered his life story. After a night's rest, he seemed to have regained clarity of mind and was open to conversation. His father, Pietro, had been a *carabiniero* in Monza before deciding to emigrate to Argentina. It was the turn of the century, the golden age, when South America was richer than Europe. At first they had travelled to the north, where the parched landscape of the province of El Chaco had made even Sicily seem like paradise. But then they had moved south to Pirovano.

'I remember how we carried calves on our shoulders, rode the wild horses . . . all you needed was a drop of rain and the land was transformed into a field of wheat. It was like a miracle.' Now his memory faded, corrected itself, went beyond him.

'The church . . . an old man in a white suit and panama hat. That was my father, using his wooden staff to push the others off the bench or touch the bottom of Doña Jacinta. It was like a ripe melon,' he said chuckling to himself.

The patio was now filled with sparrows. The leaves dripped with morning dew. Carlo pursued his methodical but utterly irrational 'renovation', iron on iron, like Pietro cleaning his gun, confident within himself that memories held them to life.

Beyond Pirovano we drove for half a day through a landscape that undulated like an ocean. Then the Luro Palace, another symbol of Argentina's shattered illusion, came into view.

Don Pedro Olegario Luro made his fortune at the turn of the century selling meat to the British and hides and grain to the rest of the world. Like other immigrants with noble-sounding Spanish names, he anticipated the Arab sheikhs. Argentines made fast and easy wealth on the *pampa*, just as the Arab states enriched themselves overnight from desert oil.

Don Olegario built himself a palace modelled on a French *château*. No matter that the good furniture, the outer stones, and even the flowers had to be transported by ship across the Atlantic and then a thousand kilometres overland. If that is how a French *château* looked, then that is how it had to be built. The expanse of the Argentine landscape allowed it to be set in an area the size of a French province. Within months Counts and Dukes from all over Europe were braving the sea crossing and the carriage ride for a two-week extravaganza of bird watching, bird shooting and croquet. Some other animals, such as the red deer, were imported specially for the occasion. But the majority had strange-sounding Indian names like *guanacos* and *nandues*. They looked rather like llamas and ostriches and were regarded as a great deal more fun to hunt.

Following the First World War, Argentina's exports began to lose their markets and the crisis reverberated in Luro. Plots of land were sold off here and there. In the mid 1930s, the estate was handed over to a Spaniard, Don Antonio Maura, a man for whom a bankrupt *estancia* in South America was better than no land at all in Civil War Spain. Don Antonio, however, was eventually to sell the estate to the local municipality as a museum.

In December 1985, we were handed a 'tourist map' by the gatekeeper. A diagram showed the main house, two out-houses converted into public conveniences and a zoo. But the house was a semi-ruin, and the public conveniences filled with insects. Only in the 'zoo' did we find any signs of life. Inside a solitary cage, a wolf paced up and down and occasionally yawned. He was very thin and walked with a limp. Beyond, the prairie, flat and dusty, led to a lake filled with flamingos, the only remnant of more exotic days.

Now not even the occasional car crossed our path and as the memories of Pirovano faded, it seemed as if we had left behind not just the first but also the last town on the *pampa*. Only once in that time did we meet a human being. I recognised the man who emerged from a ditch and stumbled on to the highway as a wandering tramp, one of the many who still roam the *pampa* begging for a piece of bread or some cooked meat. He seemed ageless. Beneath a broad-brimmed hat, a tangled bush of black beard grew chaotically from a face that was weather beaten and unwashed and had turned a rusty brown. His eyes bulged and a pair of very yellow teeth fell horse-like over his lower lip. He was sunk deep into a large stitched overcoat and walked, dragging a pair of worn leather boots along the ground and gesticulating wildly with his hand. '*Señor*, I have just seen a flying saucer. I'm not joking. You can see it for yourself,' he said, pointing to a piece of field about a hundred yards from the road. His breath smelt strongly of garlic and wine.

We walked to the spot of the alleged landing. Near to where the field had been burrowed into by some rodent, the grass had been parched in an almost perfect circle about five feet in diameter, and was still smouldering. 'I was sitting here watching a *vizcacha* when whoosh this glittering dragon came out of the sky. It landed here, I tell you, it landed here,' the tramp said, jumping up and down, holding his coat by its lapels, before stopping and gazing fearfully towards the horizon. Near by were some discarded bottles, an empty packet of cigarettes, and a blanket. I looked up and for an instant thought I glimpsed a pinprick of light zig-zagging across the sky. But when I closed my eyes and opened them again, all I could see was a plane moving between wisps of cloud.

As we stood in silence, a hot gust of wind blew towards us from the south-west, making the bottles roll and tossing the cigarette packet in the air. It pirouetted before floating across the plain. 'The *pampero* will make us fly,' the tramp said. He was facing it now, holding his hat with his hands, looking every bit the scarecrow. Then as suddenly as it had come the wind dropped, and the atmosphere grew close and dark. Over the horizon a wall of black cloud, ringed by yellow light, was advancing.

'Perhaps you should tell the newspapers about your dragon,' I said, handing the tramp some money.

'I don't believe in newspapers, they invent things just like the President of the Republic,' the tramp said, his yellow teeth rising over a hysterical cackle of laughter. Seconds later I watched him walk, then break into a run across the plain towards the place where the rain now divided the landscape with a thin veil. There he stopped and danced until the black cloud had moved over him and turned north towards Buenos Aires. He then stepped into the horizon, dwindling from our sight like a ghost.

About two thousand miles south-west of Buenos Aires, the country-side had proved more susceptible to the heat of the local summer. Here there was no part of the plain where the grass had not taken on a yellowish brown colour broken by occasional patches of wild thistle. On the few occasions the wind blew, it stirred the land into a swirling cloud of dust and pushed the thistles sideways across the prairie, like giant crabs. Overhanging the highway a bright blue sign announced that we were on 'Route of the Desert' and that for the next one hundred kilometres there would be no food or water or shelter of any description. The highway here had been built along the route taken by General Julio A. Roca and his five columns of soldiers in 1879 on his Conquest of the Desert. Along the way, Roca ordered the extermination of thousands of men, women and children belonging to the scattered Tehuelce and Araucanian tribes, before opening up the new frontiers of Patagonia. The Indians had considered the land that spreads out across the southern region of the Latin American continent as their kingdom on earth long before the Spaniards came. But the few who survived the genocide were herded into reserves where they were decimated by disease. The Conquest of the Desert pitted superior firepower and numbers against the tribes. The sub-sequent orgy of brutality, alcohol and disease annihilated Argentina's most ancient culture, but Roca is remembered as a national hero who brought civilisation to the wild lands of the south. In almost every town or city of Argentina there is a road or avenue named after him. Here in the desert there was not one monument to remember the fallen by, as if the Indians' existence had been torn out of the history books.

Mid-afternoon and the highway began to melt before us, its surface undulating with heat haze and mercurial mirages. We drove past a group of vultures tearing at the belly of an armadillo. Near to where the sandy banks of the River Colorado marked the end of the desert route we disturbed a long line of green parrots perched on a barbed-wire fence and watched them fly into the sun. Beyond the river, lulled by the heat, we drove as in sleep through the oil fields of Río Negro province, where the land of dark and dusty hills was speckled with wild yellow flowers. Around us the drills, as if guided by invisible hands, pumped the black gold from the centre of the earth. With their hammer heads and rusty bodies, they looked like an army of dinosaurs.

Near-by Neuquén conveyed the communal self-confidence of an oil-rich town. Whereas the people of the *pampa* had seemed subdued by their environment, the population here had exploited the near-by fields for all their worth and seemed to be riding relentlessly on a wave of mass consumption. Overpriced and undertaxed, Neuquén was one of the country's 'privileged' towns. Its streets, lined with anonymous-looking concrete blocks and eucalyptus, were festooned with Christmas decorations. Its inhabitants – the majority recent immigrants from the north – swaggered through the breezy dusk in open shirts, crowding into steak houses and spilling petrol in the filling stations. Along the main avenue, the mothers of the disappeared had written a graffito demanding to know the whereabouts of their sons, only to have it painted over with the phrase, 'Sons of whores'.

It was with relief that we drove away the next morning, although our exhilaration proved short-lived. The car, which had put up a more or less rally-like performance since leaving Buenos Aires, suddenly decided it had had enough. On the outskirts of the town, it coughed and spluttered to a halt. We found salvation in an old warehouse which doubled up as a garage, where half-naked mechanics were enthusiastically dissecting a vintage car a great deal older than ours.

One of them was a stocky twenty year old with a broken nose called Alejandro. He said he worked part-time as a croupier to earn some extra pesos. While the others fell on our car like probing surgeons, he took us into a back yard. Kidge bathed Julia in a bucket of water while we sat beneath a fig tree, sharing some bowls of *mate*, the herbal tea tasting of cooked grass which Argentines use as a stimulant.

'I'd like to go and work in England and manufacture cars . . . take some time off to see some football . . . maybe get a girl,' Alejandro said, as he picked one fig after another and drained their ripe bodies with one long suck. I tried to imagine him on a Japanese-style production line, regimented by 'group managers' and workers' councils in a country where excessive meal breaks and absenteeism had been dismissed as 'Spanish practices'. I thought of this hot-blooded dynamo of a Latin trying to make his way on a winter's evening in a dull pub in Luton where the men talked of spicks and Argies, as they gloated over the page three nude in the *Sun* and drank pints of lukewarm bitter. So I told him that it always rained in England and that there was a lot of unemployment. 'Ah, but you have *La Tatcher*, you can't go wrong with her. Just look what she did to us in Las Malvinas. She's got balls, real balls,' Alejandro said, momentarily scratching his own as if for reassurance.

Under the fig tree, pestered by flies and ants, we conversed about the various merits of Thatcherism. Not for the first time I found myself, an English national, trying to deflate exaggerated Argentine expectations of a former enemy while all the time my awareness grew of the gulf that separated our value judgements. Against the rising cost of a pound of meat, I could talk only of dole queues. When confronted with the disappeared, I mumbled half-heartedly about the Brixton riots and Belfast. He talked with admiration about Britain's military prowess and the failure of his Generals. I urged him to no avail to be proud of his newly found democracy. 'What's the point of having democracy if it only makes you poorer?' he said.

Sharing the *mate* I hoped that perhaps, as peace pipes do, the tea would forge a common ground, but as the afternoon wore on I grew frustrated with the impossibility of finding it. I was glad when the moment came for one of the mechanics to emerge covered in oil and sweat and announce that the car was fixed.

For two days we had driven through landscape where any contrast in tone or colour was determined not by shape or height but by the degree to which the sun had bleached the pasture. Now as we left the western edge of Patagonia and entered the foothills of the Andes we were rewarded with more dramatic change. Whereas before we had experienced heat and dust, it was faintly chilly now with pine forests, clear mountain streams, and wooden lodges built like dolls' houses, through the windows of which glittered Christmas trees covered in coloured lights. Only when a *gaucho* rode across the road, swirling a lasso at two calves, were we reminded that we were still in Argentina.

We arrived in the mountain village of San Martín at twilight when a reddish hue lingered over the hills, sharpening the outlines of the forest. After the bustle of Neuquén, the town seemed to be at peace with itself; it smelt of log fires and echoed with the sound of shutters closing. Its streets were empty except for the odd fisherman or horse-rider.

At the local tourist office, a bearded young man with pious, priestly looks sat half-hidden behind a desk covered in brochures and ashtrays.

Gravely he told us that as a state employee he was by law prohibited from recommending one hotel in preference to another. 'These are hotels, pensions, private rooms, apartments – all have had government approval following the necessary inspections,' he said, passing us a hefty file filled with names. He clasped his hands and his fingers cracked. There were at least thirty pages in the file.

I asked him if he had any rooms for under twenty dollars a night.

'Oh, I've got nearly two pages of those,' he said, with a hint of disappointment at my modesty. 'Are you *sure* you're not looking for something in particular?' He had by now recovered the file and was turning to the last pages wearily, as if about to read the final psalm. I said that I was looking for a room that was quiet and had a cot.

'A cot, but *Señor* why did you not say this from the start?' the man said before slapping closed the file. He then proclaimed triumphantly, 'The Hostería Masia, two blocks and then left. It is the only hotel in town that has a cot. It is also without comparison the best hotel in town.' He then lifted his finger to his lips, hissed and said, 'But don't tell anyone I sent you there, OK?'

Masia means country house in Catalan. We were told this by Carmen, the owner, herself an immigrant from Catalonia. She was a handsome woman in her early forties, her hair set in a perm, with dark intelligent eyes. On that first night she recalled how, as a young girl during the Spanish Civil War, she had hidden from Franco's troops in the loft of a *masia* owned by an absentee landlord. About a hundred women and children – all refugees – had huddled together among the old wooden furniture and toasted their bits of bread over a small stove. 'We were squashed together like sardines. But compared to the rain and the cold and the other places we'd been sleeping in, it seemed like home, like paradise really. I made a vow to myself that when I got older I would build myself a *masia* just like that one we stayed in.'

Carmen had eventually crossed the Pyrenees, and with her family caught a boat to South America. They stayed first in Mexico among the exiled Spanish community before ending up in Argentina. 'My grandfather made a small fortune selling false pearls and then lost it after the military coup in 1976. The Generals had this Economy Minister called Martínez de Hoz who was crazy about the free market. He pulled down all our tariff barriers and the country was flooded with false pearls.'

Nevertheless her grandfather had managed to use his cash on

the local foreign exchange market when the local currency became overvalued against the dollar and he made another fortune.

'You see these?' Carmen said, clutching a pearl necklace around her neck. 'They're real ones. He bought them for me when we built the hotel.'

Her hotel was one of the most hospitable we were to encounter on our travels round South America. It had solid wood furniture, a raging log fire, and small panelled bedrooms with thick carpets which enveloped you like a glove. At supper we were served by Félix, a middle-aged nationalised Argentine who claimed to have been born in Tripoli. He waddled rather than walked, his buttocks tightly compressed inside a pair of loud check trousers. He fussed over us like a nanny and fed us on sweet cakes and cider.

On Christmas Eve, we drove to the near-by Lanín National Park. A dirt track wound its way up the mountains through the pine forest before dipping down to where a massive volcanic eruption had many thousands of years ago formed Lake Lácar. The lake was served by a wide stream that tumbled down the mountainside, flashing silver over the rocks, before merging with the tranquil waters in reflections of green and blue. In the distance, the peaks of the Andes, among them the Lanín volcano, were bathed in light. Upstream we watched a solitary angler contribute to the kaleidoscope by donning a pair of bright green waders before walking into the water. Within seconds he was whipping the surface with a bright orange fishing rod and line, tipped with a fly of such elaborate composition as to make a peacock in full bloom look dull by comparison. On the river bank he had left a large metal box filled with flies of every shape and colour imaginable. As the day progressed he tried each individual temptress, but to no avail. His line flashed here and there like a live wire, his flies penetrated each nook and cranny of the rushing stream, he tested the shallow and the deep beneath the water line, while all about him huge rainbow trout danced in midair like miniature dolphins, before plunging into the river and making a clean getaway.

At dusk a procession of very drunk woodmen proceeded along the lake's edge after attending what I imagined was a Christmas celebration. One of them detached himself from the main group and fell behind. While the others disappeared into the forest singing raucously, he seemed to sway in one spot like a bottle in rough water, before collapsing behind a bush. He emerged a few seconds later with his trousers round his ankles and displaying a pair of torn underpants.

Turning to the river he wished it a happy Christmas and fortunate New Year before staggering off, dragging his trousers behind him.

He re-emerged later that evening a little drunker and dressed as a *gaucho*. It was after ten and yet the twilight persisted, bathing San Martín in a soothing reddish haze. One of the hotel chambermaids – a pretty half-caste with long black hair – was standing on the corner of the street, clutching a bundle of laundry. 'Hey Agustín, you're drunk again, you good-for-nothing son of a bitch,' she shouted with a look of wry amusement covering her face. The woodman was warbling an incomprehensible song between loud burps and hic-coughs; his boots appeared disconnected from his body, pointing at odd angles. And yet miraculously he staggered across the street to where she was standing and told her, 'Adelita, my sweet cake, it's your Agustín.'

The maid stood her ground, her face now set in an expression of unashamed coquetry, as the woodman bent forward, lifted her billowing skirt, and nuzzled his head between her thighs. For a moment the couple seemed frozen in a lock; then Adelita was lifted off her feet, and the two of them fell to the ground together, giggling. Later we heard them from our hotel, their laughter fading in the night along with Adelita's muffled gasps of pleasure.

Along the mountain road that leads from San Martín to the Chilean border we stopped for lunch at a lakeside hotel called the Ruca Malen, to which I had an introduction from Buenos Aires. It had been built in the style of a Swiss chalet by General Perón in the 1950s as a place of rest and recuperation for trade unionists, one of the lynchpins, along with the military, of the Peronist corporate state. Trade unionism in Argentina had been severely suppressed by a succession of military governments after Perón's downfall in 1955, and even now after democracy had been restored organised labour had failed to recover its once privileged position. The hotel, catering in the 1980s for retired Generals, congressmen, diplomats and foreign businessmen, but not – it seemed – a single factory worker, testified to the country's shifting political fortunes. It was run by Antonio and Johnny, two Polish-born brothers whose family had emigrated to South America after the Second World War in fear of Soviet Communism and with the am-bition of making a fortune in postwar Argentina. Though originally Catholics, the family had converted to evangelism.

'We are traditionalists, you see, and Catholicism in Latin America has been taken over by Marxists. They call themselves liberation theologians,' said Antonio, the older and more garrulous of the two brothers. He had blue eyes and a strong, handsome face, softened only by a mouth which seemed set in a permanent, rather sickly smile. Had the hotel been bursting with clients it is doubtful whether he would have given us even a thought. But that summer local tourism had been brought to the point of bankruptcy by the government's seemingly irrational decision to slash tariffs on all international airline tickets. Middle-class Argentines had gone to Miami, New York, Paris, London, almost anywhere in the world except their own mountain lake resorts. And places like Ruca Malen had been left to cater for occasional VIPs and unusual travellers like ourselves.

Antonio wasted little time in taking us on a guided tour of his empty hotel. 'Now Pope John Paul II, he is something else, he is a Pole after all. He knows what religion is and should be, but unfortunately he is surrounded by renegades,' he commented, returning to an earlier theme. We were standing at the entrance to the main dining room, from which were draped the yellow and white colours of the papal flag. The Pope was expected on an official visit to Argentina the following year and Johnny was hoping to have him to stay at the hotel. 'You see, I am a distant cousin,' he said, with a sanctimonious smile.

Once in the dining room, Antonio took us to the window and pointed to an immaculate lawn that rolled like a carpet to the crystalline lake. The scene was empty except for a small palomino pony grazing behind some lupins – and on which Julia rode for a while – and a solitary sunshade advertising Coca-Cola.

'Do you see that sunshade? I've got a whole lot more in the garage. The President of Coke himself stayed here and told me I could have all the ones I wanted. You see, he's an evangelist like us.' So Antonio was a born-again papist one moment, and an evangelist care of Coke Inc. the next.

Now we were walking through his empty kitchens, smelling vaguely of insect repellent, giant deep freezes stacked against each other and meat hanging from hooks. Passing one hanging joint, Antonio slapped it with his hand. 'Now I'll bet you've never seen meat like this before, even in Argentina . . . I'll tell you something funny, it was brought to me by some Jewish clients, top-grade butchers who can't eat meat themselves because of their religion. They're strange these Jews, although I have to admit my mother has some Jewish blood in her.'

By now my dislike for Antonio had grown. With his shifting loyalties, materialism and underlying racism, he seemed to encapsulate almost everything I had recognised as wrong with Argentina – a country of immigrants trying to prove themselves.

It was with relief that I heard Antonio offer to leave us alone in the dining room while he cooked us some trout. But soon he was with us again, his monologue turning from the poster of a Spanish town on the near-by wall – 'It was given to me by the Spanish Ambassador, an old friend of mine' – to the amphibious planes, satellite television and electronic roulette parlours he planned to incorporate into the hotel in the coming months. He wanted Ruca Malen to become a Las Vegas in Argentina. He would make a lot of money. Over coffee we were joined by his brother Johnny, who recalled that one of their clients had been an American astronaut. 'Did you know that when you're in space you shit and pee in your suit? Just imagine doing that on earth,' Johnny said, fondling a rose on the lapel of his shirt.

Now I knew that it was time to leave. As we made our way to the car, Antonio and Johnny followed at the head of their respective families, a mass of healthy-looking women and children with blue eyes and blond hair. They were locked in a collective smile of self-satisfaction, like a propaganda poster for the Aryan race, and sur-rounded our car eagerly. One of them, a three year old with picture-book immaculateness of soul and body oozing from every pore, stepped forward and handed Kidge about a dozen printed pieces of paper. Kidge gave her some apples in return, dried and crumpled after the week-long drive. 'They're from Buenos Aires,' Kidge said by way of reassurance.

As the car climbed up into mountains again, Kidge read the bits of paper. They had been written for and on behalf of the local evangelist commune and explained how in this temporal world of ours we were all men of sin and how nothing we could do or say would make us any better.

At Paso Limay, a small frontier post on the Chilean border, we were queuing at the passport control when I heard the familiar voice of John, an Indian-born photographer friend from Buenos Aires who had emigrated to Argentina five years earlier after leaving university.

'But I've come all the way from Buenos Aires, it's three thousand kilometres away. I can't go back now,' he was protesting.

Before him, behind a high table, stood two Chilean frontier guards.

One was fat with a heavy moustache falling over his upper lip. The other was younger, thin and nervous looking.

'You will have to go back to Buenos Aires and get your passport, *Señor*, then have it stamped by our Consul. Then you can come back here and we'll see if we'll let you through,' the fat one said. He produced a large file and began to read out the latest Chilean regulations governing frontier passes. It confirmed that we as British subjects were the only ones who didn't need visas to get across. It appeared that Pinochet still credited Mrs Thatcher for having saved him from an Argentine invasion during the Falklands War, and for her public statements of support for the Chilean military's help during the conflict. India, however, was a member of the group of non-aligned nations which was regarded as pro-communist and anti-Chilean for voting on human rights issues in the United Nations. John argued that he had gone through the border on countless occasions with only his Argentine ID, and that there had never been any problem.

The thin policeman had been hovering in the background. Now, as his colleague adopted an air of bored resignation, he stepped forward with a look of threatening assertiveness. 'So you've come through this border before, have you? Well, we'd remember you if we'd seen you. We don't see too many Indians,' he said with the slight suggestion of a sneer. John insisted he had come through the previous Easter and urged him to check through his books again.

And so another large volume was put on the table and the record of John's entry duly found. 'You see, I wasn't lying,' said John, straightening his hunched shoulders as if to emphasise his self-respect. The two policemen cast a conspiratorial look at each other and then the thin one closed the book suddenly with a gesture of scarcely contained violence. 'No, you weren't lying, but we weren't on duty then. The records show that too. We cannot account for the mistakes of others, now can we?'

We watched at a distance as, for the next two hours, John and the policemen immersed themselves in a contest of wits. Arguments and counter-arguments, interrupted now and then by theatrical withdrawals and secretive consultations behind the scenes. To our amazement, the longer it continued, the more assertive John became and the more defensive the policemen. For all their outward signs of authority and violence – whenever they were lost for words one or the other would clutch his pistol holster – it became clear that General Pinochet's faithful minions were caught in a human quandary which bureaucracy was struggling to resolve. Not to allow John to accompany us across the border would have them contradicting their predecessors and make them seem inefficient, even corrupt – something which the Chilean military's Prussian sense of *esprit de corps* could not possibly allow. And yet to do so seemed openly to reject the visible policy statement to which they had equally sworn allegiance. I decided to intervene and appeal to the human factor. Approaching the fatter one with my British passport held firmly in front of me, I pointed to Kidge and little Julia. 'But, *Señor*, it is Christmas after all. There's a young woman and child out there . . . John is our friend . . . ' For an instant I thought I caught a glimmer of sympathy in the policeman's eyes. They seemed to water slightly and his moustache twitched absurdly. But it was the thin one who intervened, 'The answer is no. You and your family can cross, but the Indian stays here.'

We had planned to be in Chile by that evening, but sharing in John's frontier ordeal had bound us in solidarity with him. I had decided that either the four of us went across or none of us would. So we started packing John's luggage into his car. The thin policeman was now interviewing some other tourists, as if we had never existed. But his colleague approached me and whispered apologetically, 'You have to understand, *Señor*, we've got nothing against you or your Indian friend, but rules are rules, and orders are orders.'

Driving back along the dust road we had come along six hours earlier, little Julia began to cry for the food and milk we did not have to give her on this Christmas evening. And that made me think of the policeman and the many thousands of Chileans who had been tortured or killed because rules are rules and orders are orders.

The sun set over the sandstone hills. The golden crust of the landscape turned the pale grey of mouldy cheese. Then from the dark emerged a crescent moon, casting silvery reflections on the lake alongside the road. We drove silently, deflated by the experience at the frontier while at the same time awestruck by the resurrected beauty of the landscape. At midnight we motored into the mountain resort of San Carlos de Bariloche and took immediate refuge in the Residencia Tirol, the only hotel, which had a sign outside with the words, 'We appreciate silence. Students, drunks and pets strictly prohibited.'

John woke the next morning despondent and resigned to returning to Buenos Aires as quickly as possible. I convinced him to spend at least a day with us, for we had rarely shared an exile from work and the city. Looking through my contact book, I had also found the name of an Argentine and his English girlfriend which jogged my memory. The last time I had seen Roberto and Pat was ten years previously. They had been selling jewellery along the Portobello Road in London in order to pay for their ticket back to Buenos Aires. 'If we ever get back,' Roberto had said, 'we're dropping out for good in El Bolsón.' El Bolsón meant deep sack in Spanish. My guidebook said it was about 130 kilometres south of San Carlos and described it as a 'most attractive small town in beautiful country, with many mountain walks and waterfalls near by . . . '

We were soon driving along a rolling dusty road over hills of rock and gorse. Only once did we pass a mountain stream on our way to El Bolsón and even then the water had been reduced to an insignificant trickle as a result of evaporation. We set off early in the morning, but the day was soon suspended in a heavy heat. As the road zigzagged this way and that, over and down and up again, I realised why the guidebook had suggested that the 130 kilometre drive could take up to a day. But just as the road began to strike us as interminable, we spotted our first sign of life in over five hours. On the side of the road, a wooden sign suspended from a long pole pointed an arrow up towards the mountains. 'La Campina di Pietro: Formaggi, Quesos, Chises.'

We followed the arrow, along a path that crossed a cattle grid and up a hill over which herds of goats and sheep were grazing on green pastures. Such a pastoral setting in the midst of so much barrenness struck us as welcome as manna from heaven. The road wound its way to a solitary stone house where a German sheepdog greeted us with a panic-stricken bark. Behind him walked Pietro, a portly fifty year old wearing a white cap and an apron. With his large Roman nose and flabby cheeks, he faintly resembled a bulldog.

From the moment we stepped out of the car, we were confronted by an overwhelming smell of cheese. The smell seemed to have pervaded every stitch of Pietro's clothing, and got stronger the nearer we walked towards the house. I had asked Pietro if he knew the whereabouts of an Argentine and his English girlfriend, but the question went unanswered. Instead he insisted on showing us his cheeses.

These were laid out in a dark, cool room peeping out from under sack cloth like huge fat candles. The German sheepdog sniffed them lovingly, his whimpering now quite subsided. Pietro followed him, gently stroking each tub in turn. 'Chisa making', he said, 'was my great-grandfather, was my grandfather, was my father. Generation after generation of chisa making. I came as a smalla boy from Torino, but now I make chisa in Argentina . . . '

I asked him about El Bolsón.

'Oh, El Bolsone . . . ' he said sullenly, 'it's fulla hippies. They growa vegetables for twoa days and then for the resta of the year they live off the *bifes* their mamas send them from Buenos Aires. They are very rich hippies, you see.'

On the outskirts of El Bolsón early that afternoon, we overtook two men with very long hair and thick beards. They were wearing ponchos and cowboy hats and riding horses, barebacked. They watched us earnestly as we retraced our steps. I asked them if they knew an English girl by the name of Pat. They shook their heads in silence and rode on. Beyond the town seemed deserted, the shutters of its Westernised bungalows rattling in a light breeze, the surrounding mountains distant and part of another world. Past an abandoned wooden cart and a rubbish tip, the monotonous architecture had been broken by a brightly painted doorway leading into a courtyard. There, softly murmuring, were grouped men, women and children in an open market place of Indian clothes, dried fruit, nuts and musical instruments. Between the stalls walked an occasional tourist, taking photographs. We were ushered into a small bar by Tania, a tall full-bodied *porteña* in pigtails who was dressed as an Indian squaw. I was intrigued by a wickerwork dragon, but Tania in a voice of half-sleep said she wasn't sure of its meaning. I asked her about the portrait of the good-looking cowboy which hung over her bar. She said she didn't know about that either and lit a joss stick.

I asked her about Roberto and Pat. Tears came into Tania's tired eyes. Then she said in a whisper, 'I think I knew them once, but they left a long time ago.'

Later, as we drove back to San Carlos, I asked John why he had chosen to settle in Argentina. He looked at me with wry amusement and his white teeth glimmered. 'You forget I may be Indian but I was brought up as a Catholic, so I can never really feel I belong to India. I realised that in Bombay the day I went with the son of the local Maharajah to the market. As we walked through the filth and the starving, people crawled towards us and kissed his feet. I hated them for that . . . ' I suggested that he couldn't deny a culture that went back more than a thousand years, before Christ.

John looked out at the landscape, but registered beyond it. 'For me what is important is not history but the future. In Buenos Aires I have my cameras, my dark room all imported, all efficient, they give me a sense of belonging – to the future.'

The Challenger shuttle disaster had taken place that year, so I asked John if he wished to emulate the Americans in their quest for the future.

'Yes, like the Americans. Forget about Challenger, they got to the moon first.'

'But you're living in Argentina,' I insisted.

'Precisely,' John said, turning to me again, 'because this is a country of recent immigrants just like America, because no one really belongs here, because there is no sense of history, because technology is what money can buy. I feel an equal, I feel myself. Try making me feel that way in Dear Old England.'

That night we ate barbecued steak – the staple Argentine diet – in a small family restaurant near our hotel. When it came to the coffee, the owner, who had been watching us throughout the meal, walked up to our table and said there was something upstairs he wanted to show us. A few seconds later we were standing in a loft gazing at what he described, with an inane grin, as his 'new son – a small-scale but perfectly constructed model of a Wild West town set among mountains.

'You like playing cowboys,' John ventured.

'Sure I do,' the owner said.

He explained that this was the model of a multi-million investment he was making on the proceeds of the sale of two hotels and the profits of the restaurant. The idea was to build a holiday resort on the outskirts of San Carlos where visitors from all over Argentina could spend a week pretending they were cowboys. 'It will have a church, a saloon, a brothel, a sheriff's office, a shoot-out, a rodeo. The bar girls and the waiters will all speak in Texan accents . . . It will be a fantasy world where everything will seem real . . . ' the owner said. He had sharply angled eyebrows and a pair of eyes that rolled demonically.

Clutching sleeping Julia to her, Kidge looked at him and asked, 'But wouldn't it make more sense to build a town like those of the Argentine settlers in the last century – an Argentine Wild West?'

The owner looked at her with a look of genuine disappointment. 'Oh dear, that's exactly what the Tourist Office said . . . but can you imagine what I would recreate – the Conquest of the Desert, General Roca . . . we have enough Generals in real life without having to recreate them. Anyway *porteños* like the American Wild West better, they identify with it, they want life to be like in the movies.'

Once we had returned to our table, the owner left us to ourselves. The memories of the day filtered back to us in exchanges of sadness and amusement, but soon melancholy took over. We knew that John had finally decided to go back the next morning and we felt the distance which separates all beings on this vast continent creeping up on us again. Opening a third bottle of wine, I jested that perhaps we should treat this as the Last Supper, a sad but happy occasion at the same time.

John broke out laughing, and his smile covered his whole face. Then he leaned over and said, 'You know your trouble, Burns, you're also Catholic.' And then we hugged each other.

Later, as we stumbled into the pure mountain air, the owner's young son came running after us. He was obese, with legs bulging from a pair of short drainpipe trousers. He rolled rather than walked, rather like a sealion.

'*Señor, Señor,*' he said, waddling up to us, somewhat breathlessly, '*los Ingleses*, they drive on the other side of the road to us, is that not true?'

'Yes, even when they're not drunk. How do you know that?' I asked.

The boy issued a delighted squeal before saying, 'I've seen it in the movies.'

— 9 —

POETS AND DICTATORS

The bus rose above the mountains of Bariloche on the 'route of the seven lakes' that leads to Chile. The trees that lined the road were more than a thousand years old. They had ancient, crumpled bark, their tortured bodies entangled in their own roots, and their branches were draped in giant spiders' webs. Beyond, the foliage had overgrown the forest, adding to the impression of a land isolated and suspended in time. Behind us, where the valley dimmed in space, glided a lone condor. As the bus penetrated the mist, the driver tuned into a short-wave radio, and asked his head office to assist him. He spoke gravely and in staccato bursts, a sea captain adrift in a foggy ocean. 'Visibility . . . bad . . . north-north-west . . . kilometre thirty-nine . . . proceeding . . . please advise lake atmospherics . . . over.' The radio screeched, then returned its advice in an incomprehensible crackle. A few seconds later, the connection went dead, and the bus continued its descent through the forest, as if through a tunnel.

We were entering *Chilli*, which means 'where the land ends' in the language of the local Indians. With its back to the Andes, and extending its territory to the Pacific Ocean like a silent offering, Chile is immersed in isolation. Whereas Argentina is South America's underbelly, Chile sits on the continent's edge like an orphan, its geography enclosing it within a natural prison. With an area of 750,000 square kilometres, Chile is about half the size of Europe and yet within its boundaries are contained some of the most dramatic contrasts of landscape to be found in South America. The country is bounded in the north by the salty expanse of the Atacama desert, and in the south by the floating cathedrals of polar ice. Our passage was through one of the few gaps in the huge granite wall of mountain, along a path well known to cattle rustlers, and where foreigners like ourselves felt like trespassers.

Only when we had cleared the trees, and the bus had begun to make its way across a moss-covered plateau, did a new country seem to beckon us, and only then did we emerge from the muffled silence and begin to take stock of each other. The seeming impenetrability of the forest had led me to thoughts about the first *conquistadores* – without the help of engines or electronics, that band of greedy, arrogant peasants had managed to carve their way through this terrain with only swords. But now as I looked around the bus, I felt that in four hundred years humanity had regressed. My fellow passengers were Chileans, Japanese, Colombians and Americans. The Chileans complained about frontier crossings – not their own but those involving other countries. 'They kept me waiting for four hours in Ecuador ... that's South America for you,' said one Chilean man. He was dressed in a pair of starched white slacks and a t-shirt with the words 'I love New York' printed on it, and he fidgeted constantly with a pair of sunglasses. His wife, a plump woman, fanned herself frenetically with a rolled-up piece of paper. But to no avail. She had shed large drops of sweat on to her t-shirt, and now her 'I love Miami' was submerged in a greyish smudge. Beside them, on the other side of the gangway, a Japanese couple snapped photographs continuously while their children slept. A Colombian woman with her young son sat stoically, gazing at the mountains as if in another world.

The bus deposited us at the lakeside and we were soon motoring in an old German-built river steamer across the milky waters of Nahel Huapí, the snow peaks of the Andes pinned to the horizon like a picture postcard. It was then that I noticed the American. He was tall with a neatly cut beard and a pair of deep-set eyes. He seemed so fascinated by the cover of the book I was reading – a history of modern Chile – that he couldn't keep his eyes off it. Only when I had laid the book on the bench beside me, did he seize the opportunity he had been waiting for and approach us. 'Hi, mind if I borrow that book for a moment?' he said and took it without waiting for an answer.

Intimidated and uncertain how to react, we watched him turn immediately to the chapter on the Marxist government of Salvador Allende and the military coup of General Pinochet. As he flipped the pages, the memory of the frontier police turning over the evidence of John's disputed frontier passage drifted back like a bad dream. I was now convinced the man was an agent. Then, as suddenly as he had taken it, the American snapped the cover of the book shut and handed it back. His expression was shifty. 'You guys must be wondering who I am. I was working in Chile when the coup took place and believe

me all that stuff about how the CIA helped finance Allende's downfall
. . . well, I know for a fact it just ain't true. The Chileans knew the
man was turning the place into a Soviet state so they decided to get
rid of him. They didn't need the CIA.'

After I had let him say his piece without challenge, the American
withdrew and we did not see him again for the rest of the journey.
But his interruption so unsettled us that the lake drifted by virtually
unnoticed, except for when a momentary panic gripped me and I
threw the book into the water.

At the Chilean frontier post of Peulla, the Colombian woman who
had been on the bus with me had her luggage turned inside out by a
customs official. He was in his late twenties, but prematurely grey and
with a face lined with tension. When he came across a couple of apples
hidden in the woman's underwear, he grimaced before letting out a
faintly perceptible hiss. Then he reached into his jacket pocket, took
out a small bottle and emptied its contents over a cloth which had
been laid on a near-by table. As the sharp, clinical, smell of disinfectant
pervaded the small room where we were gathered, he picked up the
apples carefully with a pair of pincers and laid the fruit on the table.
He hissed a little more and then glared at the Colombian woman.
'These apples, Señora, are illegal, against the law, BANNED. We shall
have to incinerate them.'

The Colombian woman protested that she had bought the apples
on the boat from a Chilean who had brought them across the border
into Argentina, and that thus all she was doing was bringing the fruit
back to its country of origin. 'Anyway, my son has already eaten
twelve of them on the trip here, and look at him. He seems quite
healthy and happy.' Her son was a handsome little boy, half-Indian
and with a mop of jet black hair that fell about his face in curls. He
gave the customs officer a large, generous smile.

'You may well smile, boy, but your mother is a bad woman. Take
her away before I arrest her,' the customs officer said, picking up the
apples again and taking them to a corner of the room where other
fruits and vegetables lay piled up against the wall.

As the Colombians walked on, I asked him why apples had to be
incinerated. He told me the reason lay in history. A few years before,
a giant Brazilian bee had entered the country in a box full of imported
mangoes. No sooner had the insect been released from its confinement
than it started to smell the pollen of the Andes. 'Within months there
were thousands of these Brazilian bees. They went around the country

destroying the smaller, more vulnerable Chilean bees, and within a year there was no more honey left. We don't want the same thing to happen to our orchards.'

A few hundred yards into Chile, in a clearing of eucalyptus trees, a package tour of Americans had occupied the local hotel and were threatening to have the same effect as the Brazilian bees. The Chilean staff stood around looking helpless as the invaders swarmed in and out of the rooms buzzing their comments and complaints. The average age of the tourists was about seventy and everyone wore badges with the stars and stripes and the inscription 'Los Angeles gay tours'. Arthur, the tour operator, was bald and flabby. He was dressed in a white panama hat, bright pink t-shirt, and turquoise shorts. In the dining room he sat at a crowded table with a group of women whose heavily powdered faces had in the heat taken on the aspect of crusted cakes. They were all very drunk on *pisco* sours. As we sat down at our table, Arthur rose unsteadily and holding up a small megaphone addressed the gathering in a high-pitched, somewhat undigested voice, 'Ladies and ladies, may I remind you that the next rest stop is four hours from now. So I suggest you make use of the hotel rest room while you can.'

One of the women stopped powdering her nose and looking startled said, 'But Arthur, dear, the book says that in Chile you have to tip the boy in the rest room and I haven't got any more coins.'

Arthur hitched his trousers up and blinked. 'Now, Dorothy, don't you worry now. I'm sure the boy will understand you can't wait,' he boomed down the megaphone. And with that the whole dining room let out a loud guffaw. Little Julia, propped up in a chair between two cushions, got such a fright that she jumped out, fell and hit her head against the floor.

Afterwards we walked into the hotel garden. It was filled with evergreen plants and roses. Around a fountain, the Japanese were engaged in a collective dance, swiping the air with karate chops so as to keep the horseflies at bay.

Along the highway to Puerto Montt, trickles of tears ran down the face of the Colombian woman. Her sadness, she told me, stemmed not from the incident involving the apples but from the landscape we now motored through. The Osorno volcano – jet black except where the snow had graced it with a frilly collar – rose on the horizon. We marvelled at its beauty. The Japanese froze it in their cameras. The Colombian encountered it like a nightmare. That huge dark form slouched against the clear blue sky reminded her of the avalanche that two weeks before had buried twenty thousand of her countrymen in one of the biggest natural disasters in recent Latin American history. 'Mountains are devils, they contain nothing but death and tragedy. They tease us with their beauty and kill us when we least expect it,' she said, almost mesmerised. The little boy saw his mother cry and hung like a dead weight about her neck. 'Bad mountain' he kept repeating over and over again. Around us there were neatly sown fields of barley and potatoes, and small brightly coloured wooden houses. But even this domesticity – the legacy of the first German settlers who had come out to this part of Chile in the 1850s – was marred by occasional clumps of petrified wood. The landscape persevered with its images of death. We passed a village or two where the settlers' homes seemed to be in the process of decomposition and where the streets were filled with urchins, barefoot and dressed in rags, chasing after cars and begging for food. This one-time land of promise now had one of the worst records of child malnutrition on the continent.

Before the Panama Canal was built, Puerto Montt had been one of Chile's greatest ports. Now its decline was evident on every street corner. Along the waterfront, the railway line was overgrown with weed, and the houses, faced with shingle, were grey and cracked. Ships lay broken and rusted and the Bay of Reloncaví gave on to a Pacific turgid and sapped of movement. The town's inhabitants slept, contemplated, gripped in a state of suspended animation. Soldiers goose-stepped along the railway line in clockwork formation.

We walked in the opposite direction, to the fishermen's quarter on the outskirts of the city in search of life. We found a veritable beggar's banquet: little urchins playing hide and seek between the stores, huge men in bloodied white aprons hammering conger eels or slashing the silvery black bodies of small sharks, their women stirring gigantic cauldrons with the demonic look of witches, and their daughters bidding for customers as if sex not fish was on offer. 'Hey, Señor, come inside . . . ' said one. 'You'll have the best in town . . . ' her eyes sparkling with that look of self-assurance which made Chilean woman among the most defiant in South America. We sat in a small store filled with flies, and were served a soup into which had been emptied the shells and skins of numerous Pacific inhabitants. An old grandmother, with long grey hair and dressed in an apron, watched us silently from the doorway.

*

South of Puerto Montt, the continent of South America disintegrates into hundreds of small islands that follow the Pacific coastline of Chile down to the Straits of Magellan. The island of Chiloé, just across the bay from Puerto Montt, stretches for 8,000 square kilometres, like another country. Of the islands it is the only one with a sizeable population and identity of its own. For centuries it remained undiscovered by the Spaniards; and even when the *conquistadores* had taken over most of the mainland, they looked towards Chiloé – a land of forests and myths – with a great deal of suspicion. The Chilean coast was the end of a world they had created in their image; beyond lay only uncertainty.

The Spaniards finally dared to cross the icy channel, and then carried out their familiar strategy of plunder and domination of the local Indian communities. But Chiloé never lost its sense of separateness from the mainland. Here, where the 'land of the twilight nights' began, only hardy immigrants and political exiles subsequently penetrated the half-inaccessible forests, clearing the trees and working the land. They were faced with a herculean task. Huge larch trees, some as much as fifty metres tall and eight metres in circumference, had to be cut with an axe. Once the tree was felled, there remained deep roots which had to be dug out by hand and pulled by oxen. Some early colonists retreated and returned to their native lands, while others persevered and settled, but only at the cost of superhuman efforts.

The Chilean writer Benjamín Subercaseaux has described Chiloé as the *finis terrae* of Chile. 'No one pays any attention to this people's admirable efforts to survive. When one of their cities catches fire – and this happens often – the Chilean authorities send them food and clothing by plane, as if Chiloé was a penal colony.'

Cut off for most of its history from the mainland life, Chiloé has developed an almost tribal sense of community, guided by its myths and legends and its continuing struggle against the elements. It is said by the *chilotes* that the straits separating their island from the mainland are filled with spirits. The most common are little dragons who skim the water at night, flashing a trail of bright red lights between the waves. Any boat that follows them ends up smashed against the rocks. The most rare is the ghost clipper called *El Caleuche*. The ship is sometimes seen on stormy nights with translucent sails spread out across the horizon. Out at sea, it crosses in front of ships in danger, sealing their fate. Sometimes it approaches the shore, as if suspended over the water, and recruits those seafarers who have given themselves up to sleep or to dreams. Everybody in Chiloé has heard of *El Caleuche*. Its legend is like the dictates of a local religion. Together with the little devils it both explains reality and pre-empts it. Many sailors and fishermen have died in Chiloé. But many have also been saved because fear has made them extra cautious.

In December 1985 we crossed the straits in daytime. Except for a ferry going in the opposite direction, the channel seemed deserted. It was a silent crossing, beneath a grey sky and over oily waters. Across the deck a little boy was feeding his potato crisps to some frenetic seagulls, an old woman was puking into a paper bag, and a kitchen hand was emptying a box of paper cups into the water. But throughout the half-hour journey, a sailor stood by the crumpled chains of the ship's anchor, gaping out towards the horizon, saying not a word, moving not a limb, lest *El Caleuche* should suddenly appear.

Once ashore, a bus took us through a coastal countryside which at a glance seemed less legendary than familiar. Its corn and potato fields were an extension of those we had seen on the approach to Puerto Montt, although here the neat patches of agrarian life reminded us of England. Only when we went through a village did the contrast become more marked. The walls of the houses were decorated with fish scales; the churches were bright red with yellow windows; the people were shorter and more robust than those we had seen on the mainland. They spoke Chilean in a fast local dialect which I had to make a great effort to understand. As we approached Castro, the provincial capital, in the late afternoon, the landscape underwent a dramatic change. As if from nowhere, a mass of black storm clouds moved across the waters shrouding all about us in thick rain. Then the clouds cleared as suddenly as they had appeared, and the sun revealed once again the green and reddish hues of the potato fields.

The town had been partially destroyed by an earthquake and ensuing tidal wave in 1960. With its population of 2,000, it seemed to have survived only with difficulty. It was dislodged, with its terraced houses awkwardly perched on stilts and its narrow streets winding down to the water's edge. Life seemed to revolve round its square, where a cathedral, painted orange and built of rough wood, was filled with the memories of drowned seamen. The local population had just finished celebrating a feast day. Balloons still floated in the air, and bits of coloured paper rolled across the dusty pavement. Through the loudspeakers, metallic and distant, wailed a recording of John Lennon.

Here and there a park bench was occupied by a courting couple, satiated by the day's excitement and now lingering in sleepy embraces. A couple of old men leaned on crooked walking sticks and played cards. Young men, dressed in jeans and freshly ironed white shirts, stood smoking, striking poses, savouring moments of imagined self-importance until a leather-booted *carabinero* marched up to them and told them the party was over. One of the youths approached and offered to carry our bags to the hotel. He was short and active and friendly. He was called Pablo. 'You can tell that *carabinero* comes from the mainland. He's got no sense of humour. If Chile was inhabited by *chilotes*, we would never have had Pincochet,' Pablo said.

I asked him what he did for a living.

'My father has a plot of land as did my grandfather. I help him at harvest time. Otherwise not a great deal. There is nothing much to do here in Chiloé except wait for the time to go and work in another country,' said Pablo.

I asked him which country was the best to work in.

'Most of us end up in Argentina. But I want to go to the United States of America. Perhaps I could make hamburgers there, learn English. Anyway it is where the good music comes from.'

When I asked him what he thought of Pinochet, Pablo looked over his shoulder as if to check whether the *carabinero* was still out of sight, before saying that hopefully one day he would be replaced by a government of the people. 'But what we might do or say in Chiloé has no effect on the politics of our country. We are too far away to change anything.'

We caught a bus to Dalcahue, a fishing village some twenty kilometres up the coast of Chiloé. It was pouring with rain and our view of the landscape was diminished to just a few yards. Inland we went past fields bordered by squat hedges, beyond which the countryside seemed to be suspended in cloud. The bus was filled with local traders on the way to Dalcahue's Sunday market. Most of them sat at the back on vegetable boxes, draped in plastic ponchos like stoic sentinels. When we had boarded the bus we had tried to sit on the boxes too, but there was a general insistence that we should take our place on one of the few seats. There seemed to be no underlying resentment in the offer, just a fact of life. The bus was divided along clear class and racial lines. On the box nearest to where we sat was Sebastián, a twenty-year-old *mestizo* who claimed to be on his way to Dalcahue to sell watches. Watches he certainly had, for they seemed to peep from every available pocket and crease. Small ones, big ones, square ones, round ones, on metal chains or strapped in cheap plastic, Sebastián catered for every taste. The watches were pinned to him like trophies, and their ceaseless ticking had seemed to impregnate him with nervous energy.

Sebastián's front teeth were missing, and his eyes were set in a squint which seemed to focus momentarily only when the bus hit a pot-hole. This happened several times as we rattled our way through the steamy countryside. The boy was anxious to talk.

'You're from England, right, so tell me, how much would it cost for me to get there?'

It would cost him more than he would earn in a lifetime of trying to sell watches in Dalcahue, I thought. I told him that I didn't know for certain, but that it would probably be more expensive than the bus drive we were sharing.

'Are we like the Mexicans?'

I said that Mexicans and *chilotes* struck me as very different . . .

'I think we are very similar. We both drink so much, too much perhaps. Look at that lot in their plastic coats, they're dumb from too much drinking. They got drunk in the plaza, now they've lost their brains.'

I asked Sebastián about his watches.

'My grandfather sold watches, my father sold watches, now I sell watches, but don't ask me about watches I hate the damn things. Tell me, do you like fucking? The best place is the beach, you know.'

I said I thought the beach was cold and uncomfortable but maybe in Castro it was different.

Sebastián told me about his family. His brothers and uncles were all working in Argentina because, he said, the wages were higher and the currency stronger. If he sold enough watches in the coming weeks he would try and join them, but business hadn't been very good lately. Now he was thinking of going up to Santiago and enlisting in the army because there seemed nothing better left to do now that the military was firmly in power.

'My brother shot an Argentine once. It was just before Christmas 1978 when we were about to go to war over those islands in the Beagle Channel. It was only stopped at the last minute because the Pope sent his special envoy and convinced the two military governments that Catholic countries must not shed blood against each other. But my brother killed an Argentine anyway. He was on border patrol up in the mountains and he saw this young conscript climbing over a fence. He said it was as easy as shooting a hen. My brother said that the Argentine's blood was bright orange like the cathedral . . . '

By the time we reached Dalcahue, I had grown tired of Sebastián and his watches. Man and instrument seemed perfectly suited to each other, mutually dependent and without a life of their own. In other circumstances I may have thought of Sebastián as something of a maverick in a world that had gone to sleep, a refreshing sparkle in a dull morning. But I was struck only by his callousness and his flippant loyalties. For all its briefness, I felt I had detected in this encounter the anaesthetised inhabitant of Pinochet's Chile.

The rain had turned the streets of Dalcahue into rivers of mud, forcing the traders to set up their stalls in a disused hangar by the harbour. They gathered like refugees, hustling for space and arguing with each other. Sebastián set up his watches on a piece of white cloth between a stand selling pots and pans and another selling gargantuan women's underwear. He looked at me rather sheepishly, as if diminished by the circumstances. We sought our own shelter in a small *pensión* overlooking the harbour. It was a dark, damp place run by an unshaven hunchback and his similarly bearded wife. We were ushered into a kitchen where under a naked yellow light bulb we were served some tepid coffee and stale bread. I asked the man if it always rained like this. He nodded without saying a word. Here conversation was stillborn. Next to the *pensión* was a small shop selling local 'legends'. We bought ourselves a *voladora* – a spirit in the form of a small bird. Although it was made of wicker the woman who sold it to us insisted that if we hung it in our house it would bring us good luck. 'It will fly only when you are sleeping,' she said with a glint in her eyes. Then the sun broke through the clouds and stayed with us as we returned to Castro, illuminating the countryside and bringing back reassuring images of England.

We caught the ferry back to the mainland and in a hired car took the northern highway, across rolling fields of wheat and flooded valleys, to Valdivia, the city founded by the Spaniards in 1552. Near by stood the remains of an old fortress where, in the early nineteenth century, the Irish buccaneer Lord Cochran had 'liberated' the Chileans from the Spanish yoke. But little else had stood the test of time. In Valdivia, life had ended for most of its population on 22 May 1960 when an earthquake had shaken the town to its foundations. First the houses had crumbled like cardboard boxes under giants' feet. Then a massive tidal wave had risen from the Pacific and swallowed the remaining streets, turning the inhabited area into a vast lake. Valdivia's earthquake was so violent that it broke the Richter scale.

We walked across a bridge to what had been the earthquake's epicentre. When the disaster struck, Valdivia had boasted one of the most productive breweries in Latin America. But the Anwandter brewery was now little more than a wasteland of broken bricks and creeping foliage. There we met Jorge, the local caretaker. Thick-set with a shock of white across his cropped black hair, Jorge looked older than his thirty years. He stood stiffly in his uniform, like a child pressed into a party dress. 'I lost a brother, I don't think there is anyone in Valdivia who didn't lose someone. He'd be your age, now, had he lived,' he said, looking at me with his dark, sad eyes. And yet for all his personal tragedy, Jorge's conversation was marked by an underlying sense of optimism. He talked with pride about the new university that had been built, about the museum that lay across from where the beer factory had been, near to the river, but most of all about the electric clock tower since installed by the local German community. He took us into a small room where a range of dials checked and counter-checked the correct time, making sure that the clock tower itself never stopped and that its bells, activated by electric current, 'chimed' with total precision. At midday we witnessed the dials move simultaneously into position and set off a flashing of small lights on a near-by counter. Then one by one came the twelve strokes, as resonant as any great cathedral bell. Large loudspeakers, positioned near a ruined entrance to the old brewery, broadcast the sound across the river. After the twelfth stroke, all the dials stopped except for one that bleeped defiantly in its glass case and set off a further play of lights. Then over the loudspeakers came the chimed notes of 'The Holly and the Ivy'. Christmas was already over but thanks to Jorge and his German friends, life continued to be carefully and lovingly charted.

With Jorge we then walked around the museum in which the population had striven to preserve its sense of identity among the ruins. Its gracious rooms stood as an impregnable testimony to many hundreds of years of cultural interchange, superimposition, compromise and ultimate survival. One room was dedicated to the Mapuche Indians; a second to the *conquistadores*; a third to the German settlers. The rooms were filled with crude instruments of war and peace, arrows, swords, axes, earthenware bowls (Mapuche means 'from the soil' in Indian), and with the sophisticated woodwork of the later immigrants. They were a celebration of creativity, a lasting reminder of man's ability to mould nature in his image. I was not surprised when Jorge told us that it was to this museum that the 'survivors' sometimes came to seek reassurance. There was no evidence in these rooms of Chile's more recent history, but it would have been wrong to assume that the museum was thus immaterial. Within it, some Chileans found a reason to live. The past explained the present and ensured a future, a broken Richter scale notwithstanding.

Before leaving Valdivia we tried to visit the university. But we found the long tree-lined avenue that led to it blocked by riot police. A policeman was reluctant to tell me anything except that he was there to 'protect the security of the citizens'. When the police were out of sight we were approached by a student, who told us that although this was officially the holiday period, the university was being 'occupied' by his colleagues. 'We're saying we don't like the new rector because he wasn't elected but we're also telling Pinochet he's got to go.' Some Chileans had been saying that since 1974, but the student's self-assurance convinced me that the dictator's days were numbered.

North of Valdivia, we drove for about two hundred kilometres along the Inter-American highway, before turning east towards Villarica. In the soft light of the evening sun, the fields of wheat, ready for harvest, were a rolling carpet of brushed gold. We stayed the night in a hotel overlooking the lake just across the water from Villarica volcano. To the Mapuches, the volcano is like a god whose satisfaction or anger with the world can be measured according to its eruptions. There hadn't been a major eruption as long as the local population could remember, but the volcano had for many years been in a state of semi-activity. In daytime only occasional wisps of smoke floated from its summit. Then when the night set in we were able to see the red glow of lava trickle down the mountainside, licking at the water like dragons' tongues.

Another eighty kilometres further north we stopped at Temuco. No sooner had we walked into the main square than we were approached by an old tramp asking for money. He wore a faded suit and a pair of broken sandals. His face seemed to have been moulded from the dry earth, cracked and lined and topped with a nose that was wrinkled and unevenly rounded like the shell of a chestnut. I gave him one hundred pesos which was the price of a couple of beers. Kissing the coins and fondling them in his hand, he said that it was more than he had collected all day. Then he looked at me from beneath thick eyebrows with the eyes of an inquisitorial professor. 'You're not an Argentine, are you – they never give you a dime,' he said.

I told him I was Spanish, born in Madrid.

'*Castellano*, of course. I knew by your accent. You know, *patrón*, my parents were from Castile too. I'm called Maldonado, a very Castilian name and one very suited to my present circumstances. *Mal donado*, not a penny to my name.' He then fell about laughing, embracing us each in turn. Then, at the same pace with which he had approached us, he limped off, head bent forward in a slight stoop, across the plaza filled with roses and courting couples.

I owe to Maldonado my rediscovery of the Chilean poet, Pablo Neruda. Our first glimpse of Temuco had disillusioned us. It was an ugly town, built in straight lines and pale concrete. After the clarity and silence of Valdivia and Villarica, the relentless bus-led drive of the traffic and the smell of diesel seemed the worst of all possible awakenings. And yet that fleeting encounter in the plaza helped to trace the first part of what was to be the end of our journey.

For thanks to Maldonado present-day Temuco momentarily gave way to an image of the Temuco of the years 1906–20 when Neruda's vocation as a poet was born. It was to Temuco that the two-year-old Neruda was brought by his widowed father in 1906. They arrived in a stagecoach at a time when Temuco was a frontier town in its infancy, the newly founded capital of Chile's equivalent of the Wild West. This was the region, south of the River Bío-Bío, known as Araucania, the original home of the Mapuches, who for over three hundred years roamed the fertile grasslands in open defiance of the white man's attempt to dominate them. The Araucanian tribes had only just been finally subdued by the time Neruda arrived. As a result of a pact, they were left to live in their own communes in the countryside while Temuco was built by the first 'pioneers'. In later years Neruda would recall those Indians – the men on horseback, their women following dutifully on foot – coming to town to sell their wool and meat in a community he described as a 'popular democracy'. Sleeping in an old cargo truck while his father helped lay the first tracks of the railway, he saw the 'first cattle and the first vegetables of that virgin region of cold and tempest'.

It was a town where Neruda was able to grow up unhampered by social and religious conventions and nourished by a landscape in which he seemed the only discoverer. In 1985 Temuco was a graceless city of 220,000 inhabitants, living with Pinochet – but with a poet still in its midst.

After an overnight bus ride across 700 kilometres, we motored into Santiago. It was early morning and the thin cloud of pollution already hanging over the city made our eyes itch and our noses run. When Santiago was founded by the Spaniards in 1541, the site must have seemed ideal – set on a wide plain 600 metres above sea level, against the backdrop of the Andes, and irrigated by the Mapocho river. And yet the plain was the setting now for untrammelled property development, the Andes usually hidden by manmade mist, and the Mapocho, a sludge of semi-stagnant water where few fish could survive and where, at the height of political repression, only opponents of the regime found a 'final' resting place. Santiago's rich live in the suburb of Las Condes, up in the hills where the air is cleaner and the flowers grow plentifully. This is but an annexe to the city, where those who can afford it escape to and where the working classes can trade only under strict terms of employment as domestic servants. Approaching from the main highway of the south, the city lacks design or purpose, its shanty huts and concrete blocks each as featureless as the next. Nearer to the city centre, the daytime traffic floods Avenida O'Higgins; the avenue is punctuated with equestrian statues of military heroes and lined with towering offices occupied by foreign bankers, ministries and the secret police. Pedestrians cling to the pavements, but their movement is constantly encroached upon. Street vendors, who once set the pulse along the Avenida, are officially frowned upon and intimidated.

We watched as a woman who had been attempting to sell a crate of apples had it smashed in by a *carabinero*'s truncheon and was then arrested. The incident highlighted both the oppression and the vulnerability of the regime. For no sooner had the policeman begun to hit the box than he was surrounded by an angry crowd of women, taunting him as a coward for using force against the female sex. Only when he had called in reinforcements did he succeed in arresting the street-seller and only then under a continuing hail of verbal abuse.

'If anyone brings down the regime, it will be the women. They do not use violence and yet they are stronger, much stronger than the men,' a man in a suit whispered in my ear. Such spontaneous comments were becoming a regular occurrence on our Chilean journey, a further indication that however resolute the regime, the country itself was beginning to lose its fear.

It was a miracle that the people of Santiago had not been hypnotised by their surroundings. Ironically, opposed political ideologies have ensured a certain element of architectural uniformity along the Avenida and the smaller streets that cross it. Thus a Moscow-inspired mass of concrete planned during the years of Salvador Allende's Marxist government as a congress hall has found its use as a 'bunker' for the military police.

Elsewhere the regime had chosen to reconstruct history rather than to inherit it. The Moneda Palace, the setting for popular rallies during the Allende years, was now shrouded in silence; one end occupied by a fleet of official cars, the other by an underground barracks of carabineros. The Palace itself was heavily bombed by the air force during the 1973 coup; it was where Allende died. But the building had been re-built and the responsibility of the armed forces for destroying it in the first place, eradicated.

Near the centre the 'pedestrian-only' streets were thronged with people, buying, selling, engaged in excited conversation. And in the near-by parks couples were kissing, flowers were being sold, ice-cream was melting, but there was singing and music and here and there the odd clown. But for the occasional carabinero patrol Chileans here seemed to enjoy the enthusiasms of any democratic people. It seemed only a matter of time before the excitement bubbled over.

When I went to visit Father Renato Hevía, the 35-year-old editor of Mensaje, a local Jesuit magazine, he had just survived a typical week in his life. On Monday he had arrived at his office – a crumbling three-storey house two blocks away from the police headquarters – to find death threats smudged across his front door and all along the walls of an inner patio. The next day he sat down at his desk and began writing an editorial about intimidation. His thoughts spanned over the need for an independent inquiry into the methods used by the police, the growing climate of confrontation between government and opposition, and his hopes for justice and peace. As he typed, the telephone rang. The voice identified itself as a high-ranking official from a ministry. It was anonymous, and grave, and threatening. The voice warned Father Renato that if he published the editorial he was writing, the government would have no alternative than to take the necessary measures to 'safeguard the interests of the state'. On Wednesday, Mensaje went to press as planned. But within minutes of the first copies leaving the printers, the police swooped and confiscated the rest. At the same time, Father Renato was kidnapped from his offices and thrown into a police cell. He was held incommunicado for several hours and charged with insulting the police force and the person of the President, and with incitement to rebellion against the security forces. He was released on bail forty-eight hours later after the personal intervention of the local Cardinal. 'The only insult I offered Pinochet was in fact that I failed to mention him in the issue,' said Father Renato. A tall, imposing figure with black-rimmed glasses circling a pair of alert eyes, the priest paced around his darkened office with the restlessness of a caged animal. Now and then our conversation was interrupted by a nervous-looking secretary, carrying letters to sign or messages. She would always eye me suspiciously. 'I'm afraid she is convinced you've come to spy on me. The problem in this country is that intimidation breeds mistrust. It's how the regime divides and rules,' Father Renato confided after she had left.

He explained that the measure of just how much Chile had changed under Pinochet was the behaviour of the country's paramilitary police, the *carabineros*.

'Sixty years ago this police force had the respect of the citizenry. The *carabinero* saw his role as looking after the rights and common well-being of the people in a state of law, with no discrimination against one sector or another of the population. Now he is responsible for a horrifying exercise in gratuitous violence. He has been moulded in such a way that he no longer thinks as a human being, he is a robot.'

I asked him if he didn't think that the Church was still privileged. He admitted that *Mensaje* had in the past been able to get round censorship while other lay magazines had not been allowed to be published even. However, he now believed the regime respected nothing but itself. 'The Holy Father is meant to be visiting Chile soon. But he's been planning to come for many years. What can you do with the most hated Catholic President in the world – that's a problem, even for the Vatican.'

In the corridor, the secretary peeped at us through a small opening in the door. The death threats had been scrubbed out and painted on again. A telephone rang in an outer room. A heavy silence seemed to accompany our steps. When he opened the door, it was with enormous relief that I encountered the midday sun and a street crowded with shoppers. As he held on to my hand, Father Renato whispered, 'It is a tragedy, a real human tragedy, of a man trying to destroy this country,' he said, demonstrating, as was his wont, that it was possible to define the man without mentioning 'him' by name.

With Kidge and Julia, I walked through sooty backstreets and across squares to where the Vicaría de Solidaridad, the human rights offices, had been set up by the Chilean Church. We entered what seemed to be a hospital waiting room: men and women with signs of either physical or mental suffering were murmuring in groups. Exhibited on the walls were photographs of others showing the physical signs of having been violently assaulted in demonstrations or tortured while under arrest. In an adjoining office, a local lawyer was dictating the latest list of kidnaps, death threats, newspaper closures and simple cold-blooded murders conducted by the security forces. Recent cases included a nun working at the Vicaría who had been gang-raped and beaten in a *carabinero* van; a student who for over a week had had electrical currents applied to his testicles and anus before being released on the grounds of mistaken identity; a street vendor who had been beaten with clubs and mauled by police-trained Alsatians while lying defenceless on the floor; an inhabitant of one of Santiago's shanty towns who had his head scalped . . . the list seemed endless and ever more gruesome.

And yet even in the midst of such brutality there was still hope, it seemed. Kidge, who was clutching Julia to herself for reassurance, was called over to where a woman was raising funds for the Vicaría by selling tapestries woven by women political prisoners. Many of these prisoners had been detained in high-security establishments after being subjected to electric shock treatment, beaten or raped. Most of their husbands were in jail too, and some of them were dead. But their tapestries were intricate patchworks, filled with colour and movement. One showed a bright yellow sun rising over the white-topped Andes, and a woman in the foreground opening the window of a blue house. Another showed a field of flowers and children in pink smocks running to school. It was perhaps because the tapestries seemed devoid of an obvious political message, that they were that much more impressive. It was not a revolution which the women were craving for – but life itself.

That night we returned to the Avenida O'Higgins. There were now only a few hours left before the curfew so that a greater tension seemed to pervade the traffic. The avenue was a surging mass of cars and buses moving across the city. The sidewalks had been cleared of street vendors; the *carabineros* lingered in pairs at the end of each block so that even the occasional preserve of silence seemed regimented. Only in one place did the excitement we had witnessed that afternoon appear to have been repeated. Outside a cinema a crowd had gathered, voices deep in conversation, looks exchanged in a communal conspiracy as they bought their tickets. In Pinochet's Chile, the showing of Charlie Chaplin's *The Great Dictator* was a major political event.

Kidge was forced to return to the hotel with Julia when the doorman informed us that the film was not suitable for children. For a short time I argued the absurdity of banning an eleven-month-old baby deep in slumber, but then I came to think on the significance of this 'for adults only' tag. Was it, I thought, that the regime, far from underestimating the maturity of Chilean's children, feared its instincts? But why then was this crowd of grown-ups being allowed in? With their long hair and drawn, intense faces, these elder students of life did not seem easy collaborators. Questioning looks hung about them like heavy overcoats. Watching them I felt that any moment they would unfurl a red flag or draw a sub-machine-gun from their pockets. And yet I knew that in this as in every other aspect of political life there was a method. I suspected that Pinochet knew full well the risks he was taking and had calculated that they were to his own advantage. Token loosening of the political straitjacket, such as the showing of a film that on its first release in 1940 had been banned in many countries and even now radiated controversy, helped to confuse and divide the opposition. Night after night the crowds filled the cinema, and there was still no uprising. In the eyes of Pinochet's apologists, that fact alone proved the regime stronger than some people imagined. Nevertheless I was anxious to find out for myself if this was really so.

It is said that Chaplin had an unswerving belief in the audience as the final critic of his art. So at his previews if the people laughed he would keep in a particular gag. If there was silence he would simply cut it out. Had he sat with us that evening he would have been hard pressed to know what to do.

The cinema was a crumbling edifice of torn plaster and fading velvet seats. The mostly university audience that sat down did so with the reverence of churchgoers attending a liturgy. As the lights dimmed, a sense of expectancy pervaded the auditorium. The opening scene had Charlie, a conscript in the German army during the First World War (played by Chaplin in oversized helmet and uniform), attempting to target a giant field gun on Notre Dame Cathedral. When he fired, Chaplin did a small somersault before falling on his back. But the shell just dribbled out and fell on the ground in front of him. Then, as if acquiring a life of its own, the shell began to fizz and splutter and to chase the panic-stricken Charlie around the battlefield.

There was a giggle here and there, an isolated outbreak of laughter, but otherwise a stunned silence. Then somebody shouted, 'That'll teach you to try and fuck the Church,' and the laughter was unanimous. From then on the sense of identification between audience and film became almost total, with few scenes being allowed to pass without some participation. I myself found it hard, as the minutes ticked by, not to recognise in the world created by Chaplin a mirror image of situations I had lived through since arriving in Santiago. I laughed too but at the same time shared with the Chileans congregated there some of the sadness and fear provoked by the film. The Hitler look-alike, Adenoid Heinkel, was played also by Chaplin. 'Democracatia schtunk' (subtitled 'democracy smells'), 'Libetad shtunk' (Liberty is odious), 'Frei sprachen shtunk' (Free speech is objectionable), Heinkel ranted and raved, in mock German. His followers looked on enraptured as the dwarfish clown raised this arm and that, and scrunched up his moustache.

'Pinochet looked just like that on television last week,' whispered a voice behind me. 'The Great Dictator,' someone else shouted in a mocking tone. The cinema seemed now to be buzzing with excitement.

On screen, next to Heinkel, sat a grossly overfat Goering. 'Tighten der belten,' screamed Heinkel. His faithful Marshal rose and dutifully began to adjust his belt. It split. Then Goering collided with Heinkel and both men fell down a staircase.

The gag once again detonated the audience. As the scene progressed, the laughter crackled and sparked and then rose into a crescendo. 'At this rate we're going to have the riot police in here before the night's out,' joked a young student beside me. She had long hair draped over the back of her seat and a pair of glasses which reflected the movements on the screen. They were perched awkwardly on the tip of a small nose. The girl was smiling silently to herself with a look of enormous satisfaction.

Now the film showed the Jewish ghetto being raided by storm troopers. They broke windows, raided a fruit stall, smeared *Jew* across Charlie's barber shop. The troops began to round up the population for the concentration camps. Charlie and his family sought refuge in an old attic. Every moment that passed seemed to make their capture more inevitable.

The audience was silent now. It was not the silence of the beginning. This was marked by an underlying tension. The one remaining gag was met with silence. Heinkel and Mussolini sat in adjacent barber's chairs for a shave, each wanting his chair to be raised higher than the other's until Heinkel's head eventually hit the ceiling and brought the plaster falling down. The tension grew as Charlie was sent off to the concentration camp and Heinkel ordered the invasion of Austria against a background of tanks, air raids, gunfire. The arrogant students of two hours ago were now sunk deep into their seats, cocooned.

Charlie escaped from the concentration camp. And as he fled towards the border he was overtaken by storm troopers who mistook him for Heinkel. They insisted that he make a speech to raise troop morale. Nervously taking the stage, Charlie began, 'I should like to help everyone – Jew, gentile, black man, white. We don't want to hate and despise one another. In this world there is room for everyone, the way of life can be beautiful, but we have lost our way. Greed has poisoned men's souls . . . '

The woman student had been fiddling with her glasses. Now tears were streaming down her cheeks. Instinctively her hand reached out and gently rested on my arm. The whole cinema seemed to echo with the sound of quiet weeping and row after row was locked in some form or another of human contact. The speech was reaching its climax as Charlie rose above the debris of war, 'Wherever you are, look up, Hannah. The clouds are lifting – the sun is breaking through. We are coming out of the darkness and into the new world.'

When the film ended, the audience gave it a standing ovation. The student who had been the first to cry out at the outset began to chorus part of the communist party's battle hymn, 'The people united, shall never be defeated.' But no one joined him. When they had finished clapping, the audience walked out in silence with none of the bustle of their entry. The woman who had sat next to me was, as I had imagined, very beautiful without her glasses, but she was a stranger again. I watched her disappear with the others down Avenida O'Higgins like a ghost. I looked at my watch. Curfew was only minutes away. So I ran, faster than I had ever run through the city, and didn't stop till I had reached my hotel.

On our last morning in Santiago we walked down the Calle de la Merced in search of something to remember Chile by. It is one of the city's oldest streets, filled with second-hand bookshops. Into one of these we stepped and found Luis. He was sitting in a corner dusting a leather-bound volume and at first ignored our presence. He did, though, look briefly at my shoes before returning to his dusting. The shop was filled with the most extraordinary variety of books, its shelves stacked with everything from Dickens to Cervantes, passing through the Russians and the French. There were theses by erudite German professors, and old yellowish charts of South America. There were poetry and drama, astrology and sex, going back through centuries. 'Have you any books by Neruda?' I asked.

Luis looked up and for a moment gazed at me in silence. He was in his early thirties, with tanned features graced by an unassuming handsomeness. Only his eyes reflected an inner conflict. They looked at me suspiciously. 'I have mostly foreign books here, travelogues, novels, that sort of thing . . . '

'Yes, but I would like some Neruda,' I persisted, noticing as I did so that he was looking at my shoes again.

'Yes, I suppose they're too dirty,' Luis said in a half-mumble to himself, before getting up and bolting the door to the street. As he turned back to look at us, his face had changed. Bathed in a smile, it appeared more youthful, softened at the edges.

'I'm sorry, it's just that I thought you were the police. Even with your accent, you never know. But it was your shoes that finally gave you away. They were much too dirty, like my books.' He shook my hand, and then walked over to where a shelf was partly obscured by a desk of magazines and maps. From it he extracted a thick envelope which he then tore open unceremoniously. Inside was a thin volume of Neruda's poems covered in a partly torn brown wrapper from which a portrait of the poet, in his younger days, looked out dreamily. 'The story goes an Englishman left this here after the coup but never came back,' Luis said.

The book was a delicately printed limited edition, published by a small publishing house in north London in 1967. It had red lettering on yellow paper and with a signed inscription by the poet on the back cover. 'I am arriving in London on the 1st or 2nd July invited by Ted Hughes. Will be 10 days. Hope to see you everyone of them. Abrazos Pablo,' Neruda had scribbled.

'Take him back to England,' Luis said, 'so that you can remember us by him. I cannot go with you, but my spirit will be there.' And with that he unbolted the door and sent us on our way.

Outside, the traffic had thinned, and the mist had cleared. You could breathe a purer wind coming down from the Andes. The streets of Santiago seemed to stretch out before us with new hope.

Select Bibliography

Amado, Jorge, *Dona Flor and Her Two Husbands* (Serpent's Tail, 1986).

Bingham, Hiram, *Lost City of the Incas* (Athenaeum, 1967).

Borges, Jorge Luis, *Obras completas* (Emece, 1974).

Bridges, E. Lucas, *The Uppermost Part of the Earth* (Hodder & Stoughton, 1948).

Cunningham Graham, R.B., *The Horses of the Conquest* (Heinemann, 1930).

Darwin, Charles, *Charles Darwin's Diary of the Voyage of the HMS Beagle* (Cambridge University Press, 1933).

Domeyko, Ignacio, *Araucania y sus habitantes* (Francisco de Aguirre, 1971).

Durrell, G., *The Whispering Land* (Penguin, 1961).

Figueroa, Fernando, *Historia de Salta* (Plus Ultra, 1977).

Franco, Jean, *Spanish American Literature since Independence* (Ernest Benn, 1973).

Freyre, Gilberto, *The Masters and the Slaves* (Knopf, 1946).

Galeano, Eduardo, *Open Veins of Latin America* (Monthly Review Press, 1971).

Graham-Yooll, Andrew, *The Forgotten Colony* (Hutchinson, 1981).

Greene, Graham, *The Honorary Consul* (Bodley Head, 1973).

——, *Ways of Escape* (Bodley Head, 1980).

Guevara, Ernesto, *Diario del Che Guevara* (Serrano, 1984).

Hemming, John, *The Conquest of the Incas* (Abacus, 1972).

Hudson, W.H., *Far Away and Long Ago* (Dent, 1962).

Icaza, Jorge, *Huasipungo* (Losada, 1953).

Llosa, Mario Vargas, *The Time of the Hero* (Penguin, 1971).

Lynch, John, *The Spanish American Revolutions, 1808–1826* (Weidenfeld & Nicolson, 1973).

National Commission on Disappeared People, *Nunca más* (Faber & Faber, 1986).

Neruda, Pablo, *Confieso que he vivido* (Seix Barral, 1974).

——, *Canto general* (Losada, 1970).

——, *Para nacer he nacido* (Seix Barral, 1978).

——, *Selected Poems* (Penguin, 1975).

——, *We Are Many* (Cape Goliard Press, 1967).

Niedergang, Marcel, *The Twenty Latin Americas* (Penguin, 1971).

Niles, Blair, *Casual Wanderings in Ecuador* (Century, 1923).

Smith, T. Lynn, *Brazilian Society* (University of New Mexico Press, 1974).

South American Handbook, The, 1983 and *1984* (Trade & Travel Publications).

Subercaseaux, Benjamin, *Chile, A Geographical Extravaganza* (Hafner Publishing, 1971).

Teitelboim, Volodia, *Neruda* (Ediciones Michay, 1984).

Vega, Garcilaso de la, *The Incas* (Avon Books, 1971).

Waterton, Charles, *Wanderings in South America* (Oxford University Press, 1973).

Winchester, Simon, *Prison Diary, Argentina* (Chatto & Windus, 1983).